Teach Yourself®

Essential Italian Vocabulary

Mike Zollo
with Alan Wesson and Jane Hughes

Series Editor
Rosi McNab

For UK order enquiries: please contact Bookpoint Ltd, 130 Milton Park, Abingdon, Oxon OX14 4SB. *Telephone:* +44 (0) 1235 827720. *Fax:* +44 (0) 1235 400454. Lines are open 09.00–17.00, Monday to Saturday, with a 24-hour message answering service. Details about our titles and how to order are available at www.teachyourself.co.uk

For USA order enquiries: please contact McGraw-Hill Customer Services, PO Box 545, Blacklick, OH 43004-0545, USA. *Telephone:* 1-800-722-4726. *Fax:* 1-614-755-5645.

For Canada order enquiries: please contact McGraw-Hill Ryerson Ltd, 300 Water St, Whitby, Ontario L1N 9B6, Canada. *Telephone:* 905 430 5000. *Fax:* 905 430 5020.

Long renowned as the authoritative source for self-guided learning – with more than 50 million copies sold worldwide – the *Teach Yourself* series includes over 500 titles in the fields of languages, crafts, hobbies, business, computing and education.

British Library Cataloguing in Publication Data: a catalogue record for this title is available from the British Library.

Library of Congress Catalog Card Number: on file.

First published in UK 2003 as Teach Yourself Italian Vocabulary by Hodder Education, part of Hachette UK, 338 Euston Road, London NW1 3BH.

First published in US 2003 as Teach Yourself Italian Vocabulary by The McGraw-Hill Companies, Inc.

This edition published 2010.

The *Teach Yourself* name is a registered trade mark of Hodder Headline.

Typeset by Transet Limited, Coventry, England.
Printed in Great Britain for Hodder Education, a division of Hodder Headline, 338 Euston Road, London NW1 3BH, by CPI Group (UK) Ltd, Croydon CR0 4YY.

The publisher has used its best endeavours to ensure that the URLs for external websites referred to in this book are correct and active at the time of going to press. However, the publisher and author have no responsibility for the websites and can make no guarantee that a site will remain live or that the content will remain relevant, decent or appropriate.

Hachette UK's policy is to use papers that are natural, renewable and recyclable products and made from wood grown in sustainable forests. The logging and manufacturing processes are expected to conform to the environmental regulations of the country of origin.

Impression number 10 9 8
Year   2018

Contents

Acknowledgements

I would like to thank the following for their help in producing this book:
Jane Hughes, Alan Wesson and Paola Tite. As ever, I am also grateful
to my wife and family for their patience and tolerance during the many
hours I spent shut away with my computer.

Credits

Front cover: Oxford Illustrators
Back cover: © Jakub Semeniuk/iStockphoto.com, © Royalty-Free/
Corbis, © agencyby/iStockphoto.com, © Andy Cook/iStockphoto.com,
© Christopher Ewing/iStockphoto.com, © zebicho - Fotolia.com, ©
Geoffrey Holman/iStockphoto.com, © Photodisc/Getty Images, © James
C. Pruitt/iStockphoto.com, © Mohamed Saber - Fotolia.com

Meet the author

Like so many people, you probably think you are no good at learning languages... yet you get by pretty well in English! You need to be patient with yourself: when you were acquiring language as a toddler, people were patient and supportive, and you were even allowed to make mistakes! Italian native speakers are very appreciative and supportive of anyone who makes the effort to speak their language, and it is OK to make mistakes. A minimum of language is what is needed, plus a healthy dose of **coraggio!**

Vocabulary is, of course, the major building block of language, but you will need to think about how to go about learning it. Think back to how you learned words as a child. Take the word 'orange'... You will certainly have heard the sound first, when first you were given orange as a drink. Then, upon drinking, you came to associate the taste with the word. Later, when you were given a segment of orange to chew, the sensation of texture was added, and at some stage you attempted to say the word for the first time, probably struggling with the pronunciation. Then you will have experienced the sight and feel of a whole orange, the sensation of peeling it, and will have acquired the idea of orange as a colour. In other words, you gained layer upon layer of associations related to 'orange'. Ask the average person nowadays what they think of orange, and they will probably reply with their opinion of a certain mobile-phone service!

Words are multi-faceted and, like a child, you need to build up whatever associations and contexts are relevant and meaningful to you. That is why we have given you so many suggestions on how to learn vocabulary, and have placed so much emphasis on learning each new word with an attached 'memory-hook' to help recall when you need it. You need to learn thoughtfully and intelligently, feeding each dimension of your learning skills whenever possible: learning by seeing, hearing, doing and thinking. **In bocca al lupo!**

Mike Zollo

Only got a minute?

Not many English speakers speak Italian, so you are joining a small but select group. You will not regret your decision – whether you are already a foreign language speaker or whether this is your first foray into language learning, Italian is one of the best languages for an English speaker to learn.

There are a variety of reasons why learning Italian is so satisfying and beneficial, but the most important is that Italian is almost unique amongst major languages in having no sounds that are fundamentally different from English ones. With most languages, if you are a beginner or just aren't very good, your pronunciation is likely to be poor – often laughably so. With Italian, once you have learned a relatively small set of basic rules, you will find that you can master the pronunciation of virtually every word that you encounter, and that these rules apply for almost all the words in the language – in other words, unlike English, there are virtually no exceptions to the simple rules once you have learned them.

For a language beginner the foregoing gives good grounds for learning Italian; the ones I am about to mention are the icing on the cake – but they are persuasive and strong! The scenery, the culture, the history, the weather, the elegant buildings and people, the fact that the country is in many ways the cradle of European civilization ... And then there are the more temporal pleasures such as the wonderful food, the beaches, the cars, and the household and engineering products (Italian design is acknowledged as leading the world in countless technological and industrial design areas).

Add to that mixture probably the friendliest, most outgoing and receptive people in Europe, and you have an irresistible combination for either the beginner or the experienced linguist.

Enjoy!

5 Only got five minutes?

Most English speakers nowadays have adopted (usually with some justification!) the attitude that wherever they go they will be understood, and a large proportion of the people they meet will have at least a basic grasp of English.

Surprisingly, this tends to be much less true in Italy than in most other European countries. Many Italians do not speak a foreign language at all, and often, if you encounter an Italian who does speak a foreign language, that language is likely to be German.

The reasons for this are probably twofold: (a) Italy is slightly 'out on a limb' geographically, and this means that interaction with its near neighbours tends to be more limited than in countries that are surrounded by a greater landmass; and (b) a high proportion of Italy's land borders are with German-speaking countries or areas. In fact the linguistic border with Austria lies considerably south of the political border, with the consequence that there is a sizeable area of Italy (mostly in the Trentino Alto Adige region) that is native German-speaking.

This means that trying to speak Italian in Italy is a considerably more rewarding experience than in many countries (where initial, halting efforts to practise are likely to be met with a fluent response in English – a demotivator if ever there was one). Italians tend to be grateful, rather surprised and very appreciative if they encounter a foreign person trying to speak their language.

Rather than replying in English, insisting on complete accuracy, or feigning ignorance of what is being said (all relatively common reactions among unsympathetic listeners of a foreign language!), they tend to be sympathetic and to listen patiently, infer the meaning, fill in any gaps and correct basic errors if asked.

All of the above means that it is worth acquiring a basic vocabulary as quickly as possible, and that this vocabulary, supported and encouraged by sympathetic native listeners, is likely to grow and develop fast. The first Italian phrase that I ever learned, on arriving there for the first time in a train as a complete non-Italian speaker, was **Dove siamo?** (*Where are we?*). This was needed because the station signs in the small stations that the train was stopping at were very poorly lit, and I was terrified of missing my stop and ending up somewhere remote, unable to ask for help in getting back to where I wanted to be. I needn't have worried – all I had to do was to listen to what everyone else in the train was saying (they couldn't read the signs either…), and copy the question. The answer, of course, being a place name, was easily comprehensible!

I also found that most of the people I asked didn't just give me a monosyllabic reply (as they often would in Britain!), but wanted to find out more about me and would add another question – luckily an easily understood word (**Inglese?**) with an easily-formulated answer (**Sì!**).

You will find that most of the useful words and phrases you learn first are nouns such as **acqua minerale** (*mineral water*), 'discourse markers' such as **Poi?** (*Anything else?*) or set phrases such as **Basta così, grazie** (*That's all, thanks*). This is for the obvious reason that a lot of the language that you learn early on will be 'transactional' in nature (i.e. you will be trying to get your needs met in some way, usually by finding something out, buying something or getting something done).

One thing that is worth mentioning is that Italian culture has preserved some of the formality that has largely disappeared from English-speaking societies in recent years, and there is a polite form of the word for *you* (**Lei**) that is often used in shops and formal situations. It can be confusing at first, because it is similar aurally to the word for *she* but spelt with a capital (which of course you can't hear!). The last syllable of the polite form of **arrivederci** (**arrivederLa**) is an accusative form of **Lei**.

Here is a brief 'toolkit' of some of the basic phrases that you are likely to need (again, based on my personal experience!).

Hello/Hi	**Ciao**
Good day	**Buongiorno**
Good afternoon/evening	**Buona sera**
This evening	**Stasera**
Goodbye	**Arrivederci / ArrivederLa**
Hello (on the phone)	**Pronto**
Anything else?	**Poi?**
That's all, thanks	**Basta così, grazie**
(Can I help) you?	**Lei?**
Who's next?	**Tocca a chi?**
Me!	**A me**
100 grammes of ...	**Un etto di/d'...**
A bottle of ...	**Una bottiglia di/d'...**
A glass of ...	**Un bicchiere di/d'...**
Small	**Piccolo**
Medium	**Medio**
Large	**Grande**
What time is it?	**Che ore sono?**
It's...	**Sono le...**
One, two, three, four, five,	**Uno, due, tre, quattro, cinque,**
six, seven, eight, nine,	**sei, sette, otto, nove,**
ten, eleven, twelve	**dieci, undici, dodici**

Although the above words are mostly the kind you will use in shops and public situations, you will progress quickly to 'interactional' (usually social) language, because you will usually find that as soon as people realise that you can speak Italian or want to have a go, they will want to find out all about you and your family, to tell you about themselves – and even, if you are on a train or bus, to share their lunch with you!

Italian society tends to be less fragmented than that in English-speaking countries, and people will often spend their whole lives living in or near their birthplace. I remember well, as a 21-year-old traveller in the country, the surprise that was expressed by many people when they found I was travelling alone and that my family was left behind in Britain!

Possibly because of this tendency to remain at home, there are many flourishing regional dialects. Luckily most dialect speakers at least understand standard Italian as well, and when they realise you are a foreigner and are learning, they will switch into standard Italian for you!

To sum up, the best way to learn Italian is to get out there and use it – you will be amazed at how quickly you climb the learning curve!

Good luck …

10 Only got ten minutes?

History

Italy is a relatively young country, having only been unified in 1870. As a result, standard Italian (the form encountered in this book and the official language of Italy), is also relatively young, not having been adopted as the official language until after unification.

As Italy was not a very influential colonial power (with the exception of a few conquests in northern Africa), the overwhelming majority of native Italian speakers live in Italy or its associated islands (Sicily, Sardinia, Elba, etc.). Out of a total of approximately 62 million mother-tongue speakers worldwide, about 55 million of them live there, and only seven million of them live in the rest of the world (most of those in the Ticino province of Switzerland). However, there is a significant minority of Italian second-language speakers in a number of other countries – for example Argentina, Brazil, the USA, Libya, Ethiopia, Somalia and Eritrea.

Italy also has many dialect speakers, but these have declined in number since the standardization of the education system, and latterly under the influence of the broadcast media. As in many countries, the linguistic standardization tends to break down near its land borders; so, for instance, a dialect resembling French is widely used in the Aosta region bordering France, and indeed for a long period the French/Italian border came to near Pinerolo just outside Turin (Torino).

In the northern Alto Adige area (known as the Südtirol to German speakers), Italian gradually gives way to a variant of German (albeit with a strong accent and noticeable local variations) long before the political border at Brenner. This is a very interesting area (particularly so for the speaker of both German and Italian) as it represents the actual dividing line between northern and southern European culture – a historical fault line that is still a division of cultures, and has been fought over many times in the course of history. The border has moved northwards and southwards several times in the course of history, and currently lies north of the German/Italian linguistic border.

Although modern Italian is a young language, it has deep roots, and of the modern European Romance languages that are descended from Latin, it is the one with the closest linguistic and grammatical links to its forebear. Many words have come through from Latin completely unchanged, although most of these are feminine, because the standard feminine ending (usually -a in the singular) has remained the same.

Links with Latin

Some feminine words that are identical in the singular to their Latin equivalent* are:

casa (f) *house*	**la casa**
terra (f) *land, country*	**la terra**
lingua (f) *tongue, language*	**la lingua**
mensa (f) *table*	**la mensa**
catena (f) *chain*	**la catena**

(*Note that Latin has no definite or indefinite articles, so the Latin words are listed without them.)

Most masculine words have a different ending, because the most common masculine endings in Latin (-us, -is) elide to become -e or -o in Italian. However, apart from this change in ending, the rest of the word often remains unchanged:

panis (m) *bread*	**il pane**
canis (m) *dog*	**il cane**
liber (m) *book*	**il libro**
carbo (m) *carbon, coal*	**il carbone**
cibus (m) *food*	**il cibo**

Some words are slightly different, usually because of sound changes that have happened over the centuries in the transition from classical Latin to modern Italian, but are nevertheless immediately recognizable. Sometimes this is because of Italian's habit of removing the final letter of a prefix and doubling the first letter of the noun it precedes (so *adv...* becomes **avv...**, *adm...* becomes **amm...**, etc.) and sometimes, as with **exercitus**, this is because of a letter which was present in Latin but has largely fallen into disuse (in this case x). Here are some examples:

homo (m) *man*   **l'uomo**
exercitus (m) *army*   **l'esercito**
administratio (m) *administration* **l'amministrazione**
advenire (v.i.) *to come to, arrive*   **avvenire**
sexus (m) *sex*   **il sesso**

Stress

One of the many factors that make Italian an enjoyable and relatively easy language to learn is the fact that the majority of its words conform to similar sound patterns, which, once mastered, is almost a 'ticket' to good pronunciation and intonation. The stress in pronunciation on most Italian words is on the penultimate syllable – so in a two-syllable word it is on the first syllable, in a three-syllable word it is on the second syllable, and in a four-syllable word it is on the third syllable.

This gives Italian an attractive, slightly musical quality which somewhat resembles Welsh in its cadences. Words with the stress on the penultimate syllable are called **parole piane**: The 'penultimate syllable' rule is not infallible, but if you don't know how a word is pronounced in advance you have a very good chance of saying it correctly if you adhere to these rules. Well-known two-, three- and four-syllable examples are below (**cioccolato** counts as four and not five syllables because the **ci** is really a diphthong ('ch' sound - see below), so the **i** doesn't count as a separate syllable):

pasta	**la p<u>a</u>sta**
train	**il tr<u>e</u>no**
potato	**la pat<u>a</u>ta**
ice cream	**il gel<u>a</u>to**
salad	**l'insal<u>a</u>ta**
chocolate	**il cioccol<u>a</u>to**

However, some words haven't got their stress where you would expect it to be. The first group have it three syllables from the end. They are known as **parole sdrucciole** (shown below with a dot underneath, but this is not normally shown in the written form):

period, era	**epoca**
Modena	**Modena**
solid	**solido**
sugar	**zucchero**
automatic	**automatico**

Another group of words have their stress on the last syllable, usually indicated by a stress accent on that syllable. These words are called **parole tronche** (the accent is shown in the written form!):

Cefalù (a town in northern Sicily)	**Cefalù**
coffee	**il caffè**
town, city	**la città**
Friday	**venerdì**
university	**l'università**

Finally, there is a relatively small group of words with the stress four syllables from the end. These are known as **parole bisdrucciole**. A lot of those are verbs with pronouns like **ne** and articles such as **li, la,** or **lo** attached to the end, but there are some others as well. Here are a few examples of those:

leave them to me	**lasciatemeli**
talk to me about it	**parlamene**
write it to me	**scrivimelo**
they live, are living	**abitano**
they build/are building	**edificano**

Pronunciation of individual letters and phonemes

As mentioned previously, there are relatively few rules to the pronunciation of Italian letters and phonemes, and these can be mastered quickly, with the result that a great deal of ground in terms of fluency and pronunciation can be covered in the very early stages of language learning – a relatively unusual advantage for a language beginner! The majority of the consonants are pronounced either exactly as in English or very similarly, although there are a few exceptions:

Consonants

c is pronounced like the English 'k' except before **i** or **e**, when it forms a diphthong with the vowel and is pronounced like the English 'ch'.

g is pronounced like the English 'g' except before **i** or **e**, when it forms a diphthong with the vowel and is pronounced like the English 'j' unless it is followed by h (see below).

h is usually silent.

j is usually pronounced like the English 'y'.

k is only encountered in foreign loan words but is pronounced like the English 'k'.

r is pronounced in a similar way to the English 'r' except that it is usually trilled or rolled slightly.

x is only encountered in foreign loan words and is usually pronounced like the English 'ss' Sometimes it is even written thus (cf. **tassì** – 'taxi').

y is only encountered in foreign loan words and is pronounced like the English 'y'.

z is pronounced either 'ts' or 'dz'. It is similar in sound to the German z phoneme except slightly more 'voiced'.

Vowels

The vowels in Italian are **a**, **e**, **i**, **o** and **u**, as in English. They are pronounced as follows:

a is pronounced similarly to the English word *ah*, but is shorter.

e is pronounced either like the short 'e' in *bed* or is slightly longer, like the sound in the English word *eh*.

i is pronounced like the 'i' in *machine* or the 'ea' in *cream*.

o is sometimes pronounced like the 'o' in the English word *oh*, but sometimes it is more like a slightly shortened version of the English word *or*.

u is pronounced like the 'oo' in the English word *cool*.

Italian spelling quirks

There are very few diphthongs in Italian – almost uniquely among languages, almost every letter is pronounced and has its own 'value' – even double consonants, which demand a slight pause if the word is to be rendered correctly. This means, counter-intuitively, that Italian is among the slower languages in the world. Most of the spelling quirks are combinations of two consonants where the purpose of one of them is to stop a vowel affecting the other one.

So, for instance, the word **spaghetti** would be pronounced 'spajetti' if the **h** weren't there, because usually an **e** after a **g** would make it into a 'j' sound. However, the purpose of the **h** is to prevent the **g** softening into a 'j' sound; the **h** has no purpose other than to harden the **g** (the **gh** phoneme).

Here are some of the more common spelling quirks in Italian – if you learn these sounds along with the consonants and vowels above you will find that you can instinctively pronounce most Italian words correctly, and you will get a 'feel' for how the language sounds:

ch before **i** or **e** keeps the **c** hard (a 'k' sound) and prevents the **e** or **i** softening to a 'ch' sound as would normally happen. So can you work out how to pronounce the name of the actress below correctly?
When **sc** is followed by **e** or **i** the **sc** is pronounced like the English 'sh' phoneme.
gl is pronounced 'ly' when it is followed by an **i** or an **e**.
gn is pronounced 'ny' when it is followed by an **i** or an **e**.
ci is pronounced like the English 'ch'. Note that the 'i' is not pronounced at all, so the well-known bread is not pronounced 'chee-abatta' but 'chabatta'.
gi is pronounced like the English 'j'. As with **ci**, the **i** is not pronounced at all, so the name **Giacomo** is pronounced 'Jacomo' and not 'Jee-acomo'.

Pronunciation practice

Here are some words for you to practise saying, using the rules you have just read. You should be able to say all of these words

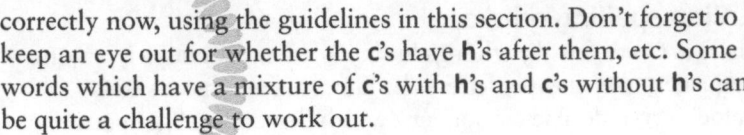

correctly now, using the guidelines in this section. Don't forget to keep an eye out for whether the **c**'s have **h**'s after them, etc. Some words which have a mixture of **c**'s with **h**'s and **c**'s without **h**'s can be quite a challenge to work out.

Greta Scacchi	**sci**
foccaccia	**Venezia Giulia**
famiglia	**Romeo e Giulietta**
squadriglia	**aranciata**
gnocchi	**righe**

Confidence

One of the biggest barriers to linguistic progress is lack of confidence. Most early learners of a new language are held back by three factors:

(a) lack of vocabulary;
(b) uncertainty as to how to pronounce words, leading to hesitancy and lack of fluency;
(c) lack of understanding on the part of interlocutors, who either correct them or answer back in English.

None of these factors should be a barrier to learning Italian, because the vocabulary is easy to acquire, the spelling is regular, and the pronunciation follows a distinct set of easily learned rules and features almost no sounds which are 'foreign' to the English native speaker.

Another big factor which will help you to gain confidence and fluency (possibly the biggest factor) is that the listeners are overwhelmingly sympathetic and (very importantly!) unlikely to be able to respond in English, for the simple reason that very few of them can speak it. So as a mother-tongue English speaker learning Italian you should find that you gain confidence and fluency more quickly in Italian than you would (or have!) in any other language.

Buona fortuna ...

Introduction

There have been many studies carried out into the way we learn vocabulary. The Swiss, who are generally acknowledged as experts in multi-language learning are also leaders in the understanding of the processes of language acquisition and some of their findings may be of interest to people wanting to broaden their vocabulary.

> **Studies have shown that the most successful way [of learning vocabulary] is when the student is able to relate the new word to a concept and to integrate it into a conceptual system.**

(Wokusch, 1997)

Put simply, this means that the most successful way of learning vocabulary is to put the new language into a context.

When a child first learns a language they are learning the concepts as well as the language at the same time. If you give a child an ice cream and say 'ice cream', they are learning the word and the concept at the same time, associating the word and the object. An adult has the advantage of already having the concept. An ice cream already conjures up other words: cold, vanilla, strawberry, like, don't like, size, price, etc.

Similarly if you decide to learn about a computer or a car you probably already know the parts or expressions you want to learn and can visualize them before you meet the word. In fact you already have the 'concept' and you can 'place' the new words within that concept.

It is for this reason that the vocabulary in this book has been given in context rather than, as in a dictionary, in alphabetical order. The words have been chosen as the words most likely to be useful or of interest to the learner.

One of the most useful tips in learning a new language is to look for ways of remembering a word: find a 'hook' to hang your new word or phrase on. We will now give you tips on how to make learning Italian words easier and more interesting.

How this book works

This book is more than just a list of words – it is a key to open the door to better communication. It is designed to give you the confidence you need to communicate better in Italian by increasing your knowledge of up-to-date vocabulary and at the same time showing you how to use the new words you are learning.

The first part of the book includes some useful learning tips, rules on pronunciation and shortcuts to look out for when learning new words. The toolbox provides you with the tools you need to speak a language. It includes basic information about the structure of the language and useful tips, including how to address people, how to ask questions, how to talk about what you have done and what you are going to do, useful expressions, and shortcuts to language learning. This part of the book is designed to be used for general reference.

The main part of the book is divided into topic areas: personal matters, family, work, education, etc. Most adults complain that they find it very difficult to learn vocabulary and wish they had learned it when they were younger. What they don't realize is that they are still trying to learn vocabulary in the same way as they did when they were children. The way the language is organized within the topic areas in this book is a direct result of studies carried out into language learning which show that adults find it difficult to learn long lists of words and find it easier to remember words if they are put into a context. It is for this reason that the vocabulary in this book has been given in context rather than, as in a dictionary, in alphabetical order. The selected words are the ones which our research has shown are the ones which are likely to be the most useful or most relevant to the learner of today. The words have been carefully arranged, grouped with other related words, nouns, verbs, adjectives, etc. and useful expressions with up-to-date notes about language fashions where relevant, so that the new language can be used immediately.

Make learning a list of words more interesting

- First decide which list you are going to look at today.
- See how many words you know already and tick them off.
- Choose which new words you want to learn. Don't try to do too many at once!
- Count them so you know how many you are going to try to learn.
- Say them aloud; you could even record yourself saying them.

Remembering new words

- Try to associate the new words with words that sound similar in English: **bicchiere** *beaker* (*glass*).
- Try to associate the words with pictures or situations, e.g. try to imagine a picture of a rose when you say the word: **rosa**.
- See if you can you split the word into bits, some of which you know already: **super-mercato**.
- Look for words related to ones you know already: **giorno** (*day*), **giornale** (*daily, newspaper*); **pane** (*bread*), **panificio** (*baker's*).
- Look for words directly or indirectly related to the English ones: **bicicletta** (*bicycle*) **mano** (*hand → manual*).
- Learn the value of typical beginnings and endings used to alter the meaning of words: **impossibile** (*impossible*); **rimborsare** (*to reimburse*); **indipendenza** (*independence*); **capacità** (*capacity*).

Write words down

- Copy a list of the most important words onto A4 paper with a broad felt tip; stick it on the wall so that you can study it when doing household jobs or routine things such as washing up, ironing, shaving, or putting on make-up.
- For names of objects around the house, you could write the word on a sticky label or post-it note and attach it to the actual object.
- Copy lists of words in Italian and English in two columns. First, say each word aloud, then cover up one column, and try to remember each word in the other column.
- Do something else for half an hour and then come back and see how many you can still remember.
- Write down the first letter of each new word and put a dot for each missing letter, cover the word up and see if you can complete the word.
- Pick a few words you find difficult to remember: write each one down with the letters jumbled up; leave them for a while, then later try to unscramble each one.
- In your list, mark the difficult words: ask someone else to test you on the ones you have marked.

Spelling tips

- If a word begins with **f** + a vowel, try *ph*: **farmacia** *pharmacy*
- If a word begins with **t**, try *th*: **teatro** *theatre*
- Many words beginning with a vowel start with an **h** in English: **esitare** *to hesitate*
- Words with an *x* in English usually have **s** or **ss** in Italian: **tassì** *taxi*
- Italian does not have **y**; in the middle of a word it is replaced by **i**, and at the end of a word by **-ia**: **sistema** *system*; **geografia** *geography*
- For words beginning with **chi**, **fi** and **pi**, try English *cl*, *fl* or *pl*: **chiaro** *clear*; **fiamma** *flame*; **più** *plus, more*

- Some words with an **e** in Italian have an *i* in English and vice-versa, or even both: **prezzo** *price*; **dipende** *it depends*; **dieci** (*ten*, related to *decimal*)
- Where you see a word with the letters **uo** together, try replacing them with *o*: **uova** *egg* (related to *oval*); **ruolo** *role*
- Words which begin with **con-, dis-, im-, in-, re-/ri-, sub-** in Italian usually begin with *con-, dis-, im-, in-, re-, sub-* in English.
- Italian tends to simplify combinations of consonants, often doubling up the second one especially with *-ct-* and *-pt-* as follows: **ammiraglio** *admiral*; **attore** *actor*; **elicottero** *helicopter*.
- English words beginning with *constr-, instr-,* and *monstr-,* lose *-n* in Italian: **costruzione** *construction*
- Many words which end in **-abile** and **-ibile** in Italian usually have the same ending in English but without the middle vowel: *-able, -ible*. Other similar English–Italian endings are:

ending	example	ending	example
-aio	fornaio	-er	baker
-ore	attore	-or	actor
-mento	trattamento	-ment	treatment
-aggio	coraggio	-age	courage
-oso/a	generoso	-ous	generous
-ista	dentista	-ist	dentist
-zione	azione	-tion	action
-ale	razionale	-al	rational

Shortcuts: looking for patterns

Certain patterns reveal important facts about the type of word you are trying to learn.

- Most words in Italian ending in **-o** (except verbs) are masculine, belonging to the same group of words as real masculine words such as **ragazzo** (*boy*) and **toro** (*bull*).

- Most words in Italian ending in -a (except verbs) are feminine, belonging to the same group of words as real feminine words such as **ragazza** (*girl*) and **vacca** (*cow*).
- Most masculine words end in -o.
- Most feminine words end in -a.
- Words ending in -ore, -ere, -ale, -ile and -ame are masculine.
- Words ending in -ione, -udine, -igine, -ite, -ie, -tù and -tà are feminine.
- Almost all verb forms end in a vowel.

Other patterns which can be seen in Italian are similar to those in English.

- Words ending in -mente (adverbs) are similar to English words ending in *-ly*, such as **rapidamente** *rapidly*; **costantemente** *constantly*. As you can see, in Italian and English, adverbs are based on adjectives, in this case **rapido** *rapid*, **costante** *constant*, simply with the endings -mente and *-ly* added.
- Sometimes, if you know a basic Italian word, it is easy to work out an adapted version.

Here are some examples showing how this works:

-ale	= *-al*	**industria** *industry*, **industriale** *industrial*
-ore	= *-er*	**pittura** *painting*, **pittore** *painter*
-oso/a	= *-ous*	**favola** *fable*, **favoloso** *fabulous*
-ista	= *-ist*	**chitarra** *guitar*, **chitarrista** *guitarist*

- Similarly, some Italian words can be converted by adding a syllable at the beginning, and most work the same as in English, as follows:

con-	= *con-*	**tenere** *to hold*, **contenere** *to contain* (*hold within*)
re-	= *re-*	**inventare** *to invent*, **reinventare** *to reinvent*

- The following syllables added to the beginning of a word cause it to have the opposite or negative meaning:

dis-/des- = *dis-*	**ordine** *order*, **disordine** *disorder*
im- = *im-*	**possibile** *possible*, **impossibile** *impossible*
in- = *in-*	**tollerante** *tolerant*, **intollerante** *intolerant*

The alphabet

This is the English alphabet with Italian pronunciation, useful if you need to spell out your name, surname, address and so on.

a   ah as in *car*
b   bi as in *beat*
c   chi as in *cheat*
d   di as in *deep*
e   e as in *egg*
f   effe as in *effective* but double length **f**
g   ji as in *genie*
h   acca as in *Acapulco* but double length **c**
i   ce as in *peep*
j   i lungo
k   kappa as in *cappa*
l   elle as in *telephone* but double length **l**
m   emme as in *emery* but double length **m**
n   enne as in *enemy* but double length **n**
o   o as in *cot*
p   pi as in *peep*
q   cu as in *cuckoo*
r   erre as in *hereditary*, with rolled **r**
s   esse as in *essential*
t   ti as in *teetotal*
u   oo as in *cuckoo*
v   vi as in *veeneck*
w   doppia vi as above
x   iks

y ipsilon
z dzeta

The letters *j*, *k*, *w*, *x* and *y* are not in the Italian alphabet and you won't find them in Italian words; however, they do figure in 'imported' words, and you may need to be able to spell them out if they appear in your personal details. Practise saying the letters of the alphabet aloud, and try spelling out your name, address and other important words.

Note that when spelling proper names over the phone, Italians use mainly names of towns: **A come Ancona, B come Bologna,** etc.

Ancona	i lunga / jersey	Savona / Sassari
Bologna	Kursaal / cappa	Torino
Como	Livorno	Udine
Domodossola	Milano	Venezia
Empoli	Napoli	Washington
Firenze	Otranto	ics / xilofono
Genova	Padova / Pisa	York / yacht / ipsilon
Hotel / acca	Quarto	Zara / zeta
Imola	Roma	

Punctuation

In addition to the pronunciation guide, you may need to say some of the following if you have to spell out something more complicated.

punctuation	**punteggiatura**
full stop	**punto**
comma	**virgola**
colon	**due punti**
semi-colon	**punto e virgola**
question mark	**punto interrogativo**

exclamation mark	punto esclamativo
inverted commas	virgolette
capital letter	maiuscola
small letter, lower case	minuscola
hyphen	trattino
dash	lineetta
full stop, new sentence	punto e segue
full stop, new paragraph/ line	punto e a capo
next word	parola seguente
space	spazio
blank	spazio in bianco
forward slash	barra
backward slash	barra inversa
@ / at	chiocciola
computer keyboard	la tastiera
control	il tasto di controllo
Alt	il tasto Alt
Delete	il tasto di eliminazione
enter	il tasto di invio
return	il tasto di ritorno

Pronunciation

- Vowels: all are pure and always sound the same. All vowels are always pronounced, wherever they occur in a word. Where two or more vowels occur together, each is pronounced with its normal value in the correct order.

  e.g. italiano = italeeaano
  macellaio = machellaeeo

- Consonants are always pronounced, wherever they occur in a word with one notable exception: **h**, which is **never** pronounced. Where they are doubled, you literally make them sound twice as long; this is what helps to give Italian its lilting, musical rhythm.

- Note and learn the pronunciation of the following consonants.

letters	sounds	examples
c	hard **c** before **a**, **o**, and **u**	**c**asa, **C**omo, **c**upola
	ch sound before **e** and **i**	**C**inque**c**ento, **C**inzano, Gu**cc**i
g	hard **g** before **a**, **o** and **u**	**g**ala, **g**ola, **g**uerra
	j sound before **e** and **i**	**g**enerale, **G**inevra
ch	hard **c** before **e** and **i**	per**ch**é, **ch**itarra, **Ch**ianti
gh	hard **g** before **e** and **i**	lun**gh**ezza, Lambor**gh**ini, **gh**iaccio
gl	*ly* sound	lu**gl**io, Gi**gl**i
gn	*ny* sound	lasa**gn**a, Masca**gn**i, campa**gn**olo
sc	*sh* sound before **e** and **i**	la**sc**iare, **sc**egliere, fa**sc**ismo
q + u	pronounced as *kw* never as in French **qu**i	**qu**esto
z	pronounced *ts*	**z**ingaro (**ts**ingaro)
zz	pronounced *dz*	a**zz**urro (a**dz**urro)

- Intonation is very sing-song, voice falls towards the end of a statement, and rises towards the end of a question.
- Stress: all words of more than one syllable have one stressed more than the rest. There are three hard and fast rules, but it is worth noting new words correctly and learning them with their stress pattern.

   1 Most words of two or more syllables have the stress on the last but one syllable.
   vino, madre, signore, ragazza, peperoni, televisione
   2 Words with a written accent: the accent shows where the stress falls.
   caffè, ragù, perché, giovedì

3 Words which don't follow rules 1 and 2 have to be learnt by experience!

   gondola, sindaco, mi piacerebbero, telefonano

Written accents are also used to distinguish between pairs of otherwise identical words.

te	*you*	tè	*tea*
e	*and*	è	*is*
si	*self*	sì	*yes*

To sum up, once you are familiar with all of the above rules, Italian spelling and pronunciation are very reliable. Of course you won't learn them overnight, and it may be best to concentrate on learning and practising one at a time. Another useful method is to record and listen to spoken Italian as often as possible. Here are some ideas as to how you can make recordings of natural spoken Italian:

- Take a portable cassette player and some blank cassettes every time you go to Italy. Try recording from the local radio, or even people speaking, though you ought to ask their permission first!
- In some parts of the UK, especially in the south, you can sometimes pick up Italian radio: try playing around with your tuner, and if you find an Italian radio station, try to record some Italian.
- If you have Italian friends, ask them to make recordings for you, perhaps sending you messages with their family news, or giving their views on topics of interest to you.
- If you have satellite TV, see if you can also receive Italian radio, and if not, talk to your local TV shop to ask if it is worth re-tuning your satellite equipment.
- Try to acquire recordings of Italian songs, pop music, ballads and so on – listen and learn!
- If you have access to the Internet, try to find Italian radio broadcasts, which are sometimes available via radio station websites.

- If you have Italian friends, try recording short messages on cassette, send them to your friends, and ask them to comment on, and correct your pronunciation.
- When speaking direct to Italian people, ask them to correct your pronunciation when possible.
- Once you have some recordings, listen to them as often as possible, and try to repeat what you hear, imitating the sounds and repeating short chunks of Italian. You might try writing out small sections, saying them aloud and comparing your version with the original.

Toolbox

Nouns – gender and plurals

All Italian nouns (names of things or people) are either masculine or feminine, as explained in the Introduction. Most end in **-o** (masculine) or **-a** (feminine), though there are a few exceptions to this rule and there are also other common masculine and feminine endings. Plurals are formed as follows: masculine words ending in -o change this ending to -i; feminine words ending in -a change to -e; words of either gender ending in -e change to -i. Words ending in other letters, including those ending in -è, -ì, -à or -ù generally have no separate plural ending.

There are a number of exceptions, best learnt separately; where possible the singular and plural forms of such exceptional words are given in this book. Adjectives behave in exactly the same way (see 'Adjectives' below).

book / books	**libro / libri**
rose / roses	**rosa / rose**
surname / surnames	**cognome / cognomi** (m)
key / keys	**chiave / chiavi** (f)
coffee / coffees	**caffè / caffè** (m)
Monday / Mondays	**lunedì / lunedì**
meat sauce / sauces	**ragù / ragù** (m)
city / cities	**città / città**

Many nouns, notably those referring to people, have specific masculine and feminine forms; some of these have been used in the following table to show typical masculine, feminine, singular and plural forms:

masculine singular	feminine singular	masculine plural	feminine plural
ragazzo	**ragazza**	**raggazzi**	**ragazze**
boy	*girl*	*boys*	*girls*
figlio	**figlia**	**figli**	**figlie**
son	*daughter*	*sons*	*daughters*
cugino	**cugina**	**cugini**	**cugine**
cousin	*(girl) cousin*	*cousins*	*(girl) cousins*
zio	**zia**	**zii**	**zie**
uncle	*aunt*	*uncles*	*aunts*
studente	**studentessa**	**studenti**	**studentesse**
student	*student*	*students*	*students*

Articles and other determiners

Nouns are often preceded by an article, in English either *the* (definite article) or *a / an* (indefinite article). There are more articles in Italian, because there are masculine, feminine, singular and plural forms as set out below. It is very useful to learn nouns with their definite or indefinite article, so that you know their gender:

un libro / il libro / i libri	*a book / the book / books*
una rosa / la rosa / le rose	*a rose / the rose / roses*
un pesce / il pesce / i pesci	*a fish / the fish / fishes*
una stazione / la stazione / le stazioni	*a station / the station / stations*

Of course, nouns can have other so-called determiners (modifying words) in front of them, expressing possession or specifying which of two or more is referred to. Notice how, in the following table, nouns, articles and determiners are set out in columns: whichever column the noun is in, you can only use articles and determiners from that same column, so that they match the noun in gender and number. The table also includes a couple of adjectives to show how they fit into this pattern.

Here are some examples of how they are used:

Non è il mio amico, è il tuo. *He's not my friend, he's yours.*
I nostri bambini più piccoli *Our young children go to this*
vanno a questa scuola. *school.*
Non mi piace questo vestito; *I don't like this dress; I prefer*
preferisco quella gonna. *that skirt.*

meaning	masculine singular	feminine singular	masculine plural	feminine plural
child / children	bambino	bambina	bambini	bambine
father(s) +mother(s)	padre	madre	padri	madri
old	vecchio	vecchia	vecchi	vecchie
young	giovane	giovane	giovani	giovani
the	il / l' / lo	la / l'	i / gli	le
a/an; some (in pl)	un / uno	una / un'	dei / degli	delle
my	il mio	la mia	i miei	le mie
your (fam)	il tuo	la tua	i tuoi	le tue
his / her / its / your (form)	il suo	la sua	i suoi	le sue
our	il nostro	la nostra	i nostri	le nostre
your	il vostro	la vostra	i vostri	le vostre
their	il loro	la loro	i loro	le loro
this/these	questo	questa	questi	queste
that/those	quel / quell' / quello	quella / quell'	quei / quegli	quelle

Adjectives

Adjectives are describing words which add information about nouns. They have to match the noun in gender and number, so they also follow the pattern set out in the previous table. Thus, in masculine form most adjectives end in -o, and in feminine form most end in -a; adjectives that end in -e can be used either with a masculine or a feminine noun without change; there are several other possible adjective endings. All adjectives form their plural according to the same pattern as nouns.

Unlike English, Italian usually places adjectives just after the noun they describe, but a few can go in front. They can also be used in other situations, such as after the verb *to be*.

il giardino grande	*the large garden*
la casa piccola	*the small house*
i meloni maturi	*the ripe melons*
le biciclette costose	*the expensive bikes*
il ragazzo è grasso	*the boy is fat*
le mele sono deliziose	*the apples are delicious*

The table on the preceding page shows how a couple of adjectives fit into the pattern of possible forms for nouns, adjectives, articles and determiners.

It is worth learning a few set phrases to help you remember the need for agreement and some typical endings.

masc. singular: **un cavallo nero; il canal grande; questo libro interessante; il tuo vecchio amico**

fem. singular: **una casa bianca; l'isola bella; quella ragazza alta; la nostra amica intelligente**

masc. plural: **dei vini rossi; gli agenti segreti; quei ragazzi stupidi; i miei amici giovani**

fem. plural: **le donne eleganti; le terre fertili; queste pere mature; le loro case moderne**

Here is a list of useful adjectives for describing people; remember, those ending in **-o** change to **-a** for the feminine form, and plurals are formed as in the table on the preceding page; one or two are invariable (inv.), i.e. the same form is used for masculine and feminine:

tall / big	alto	*short*	basso
thin	magro	*fat*	grasso
old	vecchio / anziano	*young*	giovane
happy (contented)	contento	*sad*	triste
happy (nature)	felice / allegro	*unhappy*	infelice
quiet / shy	tranquillo	*open*	aperto
relaxed / laid back	rilassato	*stressed*	stressato
nice, pleasant	simpatico	*nasty*	antipatico
kind	gentile	*unhelpful*	poco disponibile
self-centred / egoistic	egoista (inv.)	*considerate / helpful*	premuroso
sporty / active	sportivo	*lazy*	pigro
good looking	bello	*ugly*	brutto
outstanding / exceptional	eccezionale	*ordinary / unremarkable*	ordinario / mediocre
smart	elegante	*scruffy*	trasandato
well-behaved	beneducato	*naughty*	cattivo
polite	educato	*rude*	maleducato

The following adjectives can be used to describe things:

old	vecchio	*new*	nuovo
good	buono	*bad*	cattivo
cheap	a buon mercato	*expensive*	caro
fast	veloce	*slow*	lento
in good condition	in buone condizioni	*damaged*	in cattive condizioni

flimsy	poco solido	*solid*	solido
rough	ruvido	*smooth*	liscio
shiny	lucido	*matt*	opaco
nice	piacevole	*horrible*	orribile
soft	morbido	*hard*	duro
interesting	interessante	*boring*	noioso

Often, we use adjectives to compare one thing or person with another, or with all others. To say something is …-*er* than another, we use the comparative form of the adjective, and to say it is the …-*est*, we use the superlative form. The comparative of most Italian adjectives is formed by simply putting **più** in front of the adjective, and the superlative uses **il/la/i/le più** in front of the adjective. Some examples can be seen in the following table. The Italian adjectives for *big*, *small*, *good* and *bad* can either be formed as described, or using special forms as given at the beginning of the table below.

adjective		comparative		superlative	
big	grande grandi	*bigger*	maggiore maggiori	*biggest*	il/la maggiore i/le maggiori
small	piccolo/a piccoli/e	*smaller*	minore minori	*smallest*	il/la minore i/le minori
good	buono/a buoni/e	*better*	migliore migliori	*best*	il/la migliore i/le migliori
bad	cattivo/a cattivi/e	*worse*	peggiore peggiori	*worse*	il/la peggiore i/le peggiori
ugly	brutto/a/ brutti/e	*uglier*	più brutto/a più brutti/e	*ugliest*	il più brutto/ la più brutta/ i più brutti/ le più brutte
useful	utile	*more useful*	più utile	*most useful*	il più utile la più utile i più utili le più utili

Insight

Italian is an INFLECTED language. This is a language where groups of words 'agree' with each other and share similar endings.

- For instance, a group of feminine, masculine, etc. words all need to have endings that go with each other.
- So if you have a feminine or plural (or both!) noun, the adjective(s) that follow it will also have to have feminine endings.

Verbs – infinitives and present tense

Verbs are words which describe actions, including abstract states or changes. Most verb forms tell you who is doing the action and when it is done, as well as what is being done (the www address of the verb!). Whilst in English, the who idea is expressed mostly by a person word (*I, you, he, she, it, we, they*) in front of the verb, in Italian the verb ending is enough to show this, and person words (subject pronouns) are only used when clarification or emphasis is needed. The subject pronouns are included in the tables below just for clarity. The verb endings also show when the action is done – past, present or future. Here are examples of the three main types of Italian verb in the present tense. The headings of the tables show the infinitive of the verb – the part of the verb without the person ending and the form found in dictionaries and wordlists meaning 'to …'.

pronoun	**parlare** (infinitive)	*to speak*
io	parlo	*I speak*
tu*	parli	*you speak* (familiar)
lui / lei	parla	*he / she speaks*
		it speaks
Lei*		*you speak* (formal)
noi	parliamo	*we speak*
voi	parlate	*you speak* (familiar plural)
loro	parlano	*they speak*
Loro*		*you speak* (formal plural)

pronoun	**vendere** (infinitive)	*to sell*
io	vendo	*I sell*
tu*	vendi	*you sell* (familiar)
lui / lei	vende	*he / she sells*
		it sells
Lei*		*you sell* (formal)
noi	vendiamo	*we sell*
voi	vendete	*you sell* (familiar plural)
loro	vendono	*they sell*
Loro*		*you sell* (formal plural)

pronoun	**partire** (infinitive)	*to leave*
io	parto	*I leave*
tu*	parti	*you leave* (familiar)
lui / lei	parte	*he / she leaves*
		it leaves
Lei*		*you leave* (formal)
noi	partiamo	*we leave*
voi	partite	*you leave* (familiar plural)
loro	partono	*they leave*
Loro*		*you leave* (formal plural)

* **Lei** and **Loro** are the formal or polite ways of saying *you*, singular and plural. For historical reasons, they are used with the he/she/it form of the verb. The informal or familiar words for *you* are **tu** and **voi**. In most cases, strangers will address you as **Lei**, though when speaking to friends and younger people, **tu** is used. If in doubt, use **Lei** until and unless invited to use **tu**. In the plural, **voi** tends to be used for both familiar and formal.

Throughout this book when verb forms are translated, *you* is translated as either **tu** or **Lei**, depending on which is most likely for the expression translated; sometimes both are given, first the **tu** form, then the **Lei** form.

The *I* form is known as the first person singular, *you* as the second person singular, *he*, *she*, *it* as the third person singular, *we* as the first person plural, *you* (more than one person) as the second person plural, and *they* as the third person plural.

It is useful to learn these verb patterns by heart so that using them and choosing the correct one becomes automatic.

Here are the patterns for a few useful irregular verbs in the present tense:

essere*	stare*	avere	andare	fare
to be	*to be*	*to have*	*to go*	*to do*
sono	sto	ho	vado	faccio
sei	stai	hai	vai	fai
è	sta	ha	va	fa
siamo	stiamo	abbiamo	andiamo	facciamo
siete	state	avete	andate	fate
sono	stanno	hanno	vanno	fanno

There are two verbs for *to be* in Italian: **essere** is used for permanent notions, often describing the essence of something or somebody; **stare** is used to describe what state somebody or something is in.

Here are the infinitives and first person (*I* form) of some other useful verbs. Note how the *I* form always ends in **-o**. In most cases, you can probably work out the other forms for yourself, but because some are less predictable (irregular) it is worth checking them in a good dictionary, grammar book or verb book.

to answer	**rispondere, rispondo**
to arrive	**arrivare, arrivo**
to ask	**domandare, domando**
to be able to	**potere, posso**
to bring / fetch	**portare, porto**
to call (phone)	**chiamare, chiamo**

to cancel	**cancellare, cancello**
to find	**trovare, trovo**
to forget	**dimenticare, dimentico**
to give	**dare, do**
to go in	**entrare, entro**
to go out	**uscire, esco**
to have to	**dovere, devo**
to know (a person, place)	**conoscere, conosco**
to know (a fact, how to ...)	**sapere, so**
to leave	**partire, parto**
to look for	**cercare, cerco**
to need	**aver(e) bisogno di, ho bisogno di**
to put	**mettere, metto**
to regret	**essere desolato per, sono desolato per**
to remember	**ricordare, ricordo**
to reserve / book	**prenotare, prenoto**
to see	**vedere, vedo**
to take	**prendere, prendo**
to want	**volere, voglio**
to write	**scrivere, scrivo**

Reflexive verbs

Reflexive verbs have a special 'person word' in front of them to describe actions which 'bounce back', affecting the person doing the action. In English, reflexive verbs have a 'self' word attached, i.e. *I wash myself*. Here is a typical reflexive verb set out in full; remember that the subject pronoun (in the first column) is not usually needed, but the reflexive pronoun (in the second column) is always used.

subject pronoun	reflexive pronoun	lavarsi (infinitive)	*to wash oneself*
io	mi	lavo	*I wash myself*
tu	ti	lavi	*you wash yourself* (familiar)
lui / lei	si	lava	*he / she washes himself / herself*
Lei			*you wash yourself* (formal)
noi	ci	laviamo	*we wash ourselves*
voi	vi	lavate	*you wash yourselves* (familiar plural)
loro	si	lavano	*they wash themselves*
Loro			*you wash yourselves* (formal plural)

Here are some more useful reflexive verbs. Notice the **si** attached to the end of the infinitive, which reminds you that the verb is reflexive. You will see that many reflexive verbs describe everyday routine actions we do to ourselves. The first person form of each verb is also given.

to wake up	svegliarsi	*I wake up*	mi sveglio
to get up	alzarsi	*I get up*	mi alzo
to wash oneself	lavarsi	*I wash myself*	mi lavo
to dress oneself	vestirsi	*I get dressed*	mi vesto
to have a shave	farsi la barba	*I have a shave*	mi faccio la barba
to comb one's hair	pettinarsi	*I comb my hair*	mi pettino
to put on make-up	truccarsi	*I put on make-up*	mi trucco
to have a bath	farsi il bagno	*I have a bath*	mi faccio il bagno
to go to sleep	addormentarsi	*I go to sleep*	mi addor-mento
to be called	chiamarsi	*I am called*	mi chiamo

The reflexive form of some other verbs is used to express the idea of *each other*: **ci vediamo ogni giorno** *we see each other every day.*

Talking about the past

Verbs have past tense forms to indicate actions which have already been done. There are two main past tenses in Italian: the perfect and the imperfect. The perfect is formed with the present tense of **avere** or **essere** and the past participle of the verb. The imperfect is formed by adding an ending to the stem of the infinitive. As an example, here are the imperfect and perfect tenses of **parlare** *to speak*.

tense	use	example	endings
perfect	single, completed actions in the distant or recent past	*I spoke, I have spoken*	ho parlato hai parlato ha parlato abbiamo parlato avete parlato hanno parlato
imperfect	ongoing, repeated actions and descriptions	*I was speaking, I used to speak*	parlavo parlavi parlava parlavamo parlavate parlavano

As you can see, for single, completed actions at a specific time in the past, you use the perfect tense (there is another tense with a similar use, but in spoken Italian most people use the perfect). You use the imperfect tense when you are talking about something that was happening, or used to happen, or for descriptions in the past.

Here are ten useful verbs in the perfect; note that some are based on the present tense of **avere**, others on the present tense of **essere**. As a rule, use **essere** with all reflexive verbs and with most verbs of movement. In case of doubt, the dictionary will give you the information.

infinitive	meaning	perfect tense	meaning
andare	*to go*	sono, sei, è andato/a siamo, siete, sono andati/e	*I went etc.*
venire	*to come*	sono, sei, è venuto/a siamo, siete, sono venuti/e	*I came etc.*
entrare	*to go in*	sono, sei, è entrato/a siamo, siete, sono entrati/e	*I entered etc.*
uscire	*to go out*	sono, sei, è uscito/a siamo, siete, sono usciti/e	*I went out etc.*
svegliarsi	*to wake up*	mi sono, ti sei, si è svegliato/a ci siamo, vi siete, si sono svegliati/e	*I woke up etc.*
alzarsi	*to get up*	mi sono, ti sei, si è alzato/a ci siamo, vi siete, si sono alzati/e	*I got up etc.*
divertirsi	*to enjoy* *yourself*	mi sono, ti sei, si è divertito/a ci siamo, vi siete, si sono divertiti/e	*I enoyed* *myself etc.*
mangiare	*to eat*	ho, hai, ha, abbiamo, avete, hanno mangiato	*I ate etc.*
bere	*to drink*	ho, hai, ha, abbiamo, avete, hanno bevuto	*I drank etc.*
prendere	*to take*	ho, hai, ha, abbiamo, avete, hanno preso	*I took etc.*

Here are 15 useful verbs in the imperfect tense: only the first few are given in full, since, once you have the first person (*I* form), the remaining forms follow predictably:

I was etc.	ero, eri, era, eravamo, eravate, erano
I had etc.	avevo, avevi, aveva, avevamo, avevate, avevano
I was going etc.	andavo, andavi, andava, andavamo, andavate, andavano
I could etc.	potevo, potevi, poteva, potevamo, potevate, potevano
I was leaving etc.	partivo, partivi, partiva, partivamo, partivate, partivano

I was doing **facevo**, *I was working* **lavoravo**, *I was studying*
studiavo, *I was eating* **mangiavo**, *I was enjoying myself*
mi divertivo, *I used to live* **vivevo**, *I used to get up* **mi alzavo**,
I used to see **vedevo**, *I used to want* **volevo**, *I used to
know* **sapevo**.

Note the -v- in every form of the imperfect – the distinguishing
feature of this tense.

Talking about the future

The future tense is formed by adding the appropriate endings
to the whole infinitive or an adapted form of it. Therefore, its
distinguishing feature is always an -r- before the appropriate
ending. The endings are the same for all verbs without exception.

parlerò, parlerai, parlerà, parleremo, parlerete, parleranno

Here are some of the most commonly used verbs in the future
tense; note that some have slight spelling changes to the infinitive,
though the endings are all the same as those shown previously;
only the first person form is given – you can work out the others
from the pattern above.

to go	**andare**	I will go	**andrò**
to arrive	**arrivare**	I will arrive	**arriverò**
to know	**sapere**	I will know	**saprò**
to want	**volere**	I will want	**vorrò**
to go out	**uscire**	I will go out	**uscirò**
to put	**mettere**	I will put	**metterò**
to have	**avere**	I will have	**avrò**
to come	**venire**	I will come	**verrò**
to say	**dire**	I will say	**dirò**
to do	**fare**	I will do	**farò**

Here are some useful phrases in the future tense:

I will go – will you be going to the meeting?	**Io ci andrò; tu ci andrai alla riunione?**
I will do it. Will you do it?	**Lo farò io. Lo farai tu?**
Will you take the bus?	**Prenderai l'autobus?**
How will you go?	**Come andrai?**
When will you arrive?	**A che ora arriverai?**
When will you leave?	**Quando partirai?**
What will the weather be like?	**Che tempo farà?**
How much will it cost?	**Quanto costerà?**
Will it be suitable for children?	**Sarà adatto ai bambini?**
What will he do?	**Che farà lui?**
What will he have to drink?	**Che prenderà lui da bere?**
What will you take?	**Che cosa porterai?**
When will it be?	**Quando sarà?**
Is it going to rain? Or will it snow?	**Pioverà, o nevicherà?**
Will it be fine?	**Farà bel tempo?**
Will there be much traffic?	**Ci sarà molto traffico?**
There will be a lot of work.	**Ci sarà molto lavoro.**

Conditional and subjunctives

The conditional form of the verb is used to express wishes and possibilities. The endings are the same for all verbs.

farei, faresti, farebbe, faremmo, fareste, farebbero

You may have spotted that, as with the future, the ending is added to a stem based on the infinitive, therefore all forms have an -r- in them. Here are some useful expressions:

to prefer	**preferire**	**Preferiresti un caffè?**
		Would you prefer a coffee?
to want	**volere**	**Vorrei andare al bar.**
		I would like to go to the bar.
to like	**piacere**	**Ti piacerebbe un aperitivo?**
		Would you like an aperitif?
to be able to	**potere**	**Lei potrebbe partire domani.**
		She could leave tomorrow.
to go	**andare**	**Andremmo se fosse possibile.**
		We would go if it were possible.
to have	**avere**	**Avresti abbastanza tempo?**
		Would you have enough time?
to be	**essere**	**Voi tutti sareste benvenuti.**
		You would all be welcome.
to do	**fare**	**Lo farebbero domani.**
		They would do it tomorrow.

The subjunctive is a special verb form used where there is doubt or uncertainty, and for some command forms; it has its own forms and endings. Here are the endings of the present and imperfect subjunctive of the verb essere. Check regular -are, -ere, -ire subjunctive endings in a grammar or verb book.

sia, sia, sia, siamo, siate, siano
fossi, fossi, fosse, fossimo, foste, fossero

Here are some useful expressions using the subjunctive:

I think he is tired.	Credo che lui **sia** stanco.
He thought you were there.	Pensava che tu ci **fossi.**
Don't do that!	Non **faccia** così!
Speak more slowly, please!	**Parli** più piano, per favore!
Give me a kilo of sugar, please.	Mi **dia** un chilo di zucchero, per favore.
Tell me, where is the post office?	Mi **dica**, dov'è l'ufficio postale?
I didn't want you to go out.	Non volevo che tu **uscissi.**
I am waiting for the train to arrive.	Aspetto che **arrivi** il treno.
It seems to us that the price has gone up.	Ci sembra che il prezzo **sia aumentato.**

Negative expressions – saying you don't!

The Italian word **no** means *no* and **non** is used for *not*. Other negative expressions are given below, and **non** is used in front of the verb to introduce them. These negative expressions can also be used by themselves in front of the verb. Here are some examples.

I don't eat meat, I don't like it.	**Non mangio carne, non mi piace.**
No, I don't want to go out.	**No, non voglio uscire.**
He has nothing. / He hasn't got anything.	**Non ha niente.**
It is not worth anything.	**Non vale niente.**
She saw nobody.	**Non ha visto nessuno.**

No one goes to that shop.	**Nessuno va a quel negozio.**
We never work at home.	**Non lavoriamo mai a casa.**
I never go by bus.	**Mai prendo l'autobus.**
I broke no windows.	**Non ho rotto nessuna finestra.**
He has neither family nor friends.	**Non ha né famiglia né amici.**

Here are some further useful examples of negative expressions.

My friend doesn't have a car.	**Il mio amico non ha una macchina.**
I don't have a bike.	**Non ho una bicicletta.**
I don't watch telly.	**Non guardo la tivù.**
I don't smoke.	**Non fumo.**
I don't go there any more.	**Non ci vado più.**
I won't see him / her any more.	**Non lo/la vedrò più.**
I don't play any more.	**Non gioco più.**
Didn't you book a table?	**Non hai prenotato un tavolo?**
No, they didn't answer the phone.	**No, non hanno risposto al telefono.**
Didn't you get to the bank?	**Non sei arrivato alla banca?**
No, it wasn't open.	**No, non era aperta.**
Didn't you speak to him?	**Non hai parlato con lui?**
Didn't you buy tickets for the match?	**Non hai comprato dei biglietti per la partita?**
No, there weren't any left.	**No, non c'erano più.**
Didn't you see your friend?	**Non hai visto il tuo amico?**
No, he wasn't in.	**No, non c'era.**
Don't walk on the grass!	**Non calpestare l'erba!**
No entry	**Vietato l'accesso**
No exit	**Vietato uscire**
No admission for children	**Vietato l'accesso ai bambini**
No smoking	**Vietato fumare**
No dogs	**Vietato l'accesso ai cani**
Don't do it!	**Non lo faccia!**
Don't eat it!	**Non lo mangi!**
Don't open the window.	**Non aprire la finestra.**
Don't cross the road.	**Vietato attraversare la strada.**

.... is not allowed / permitted	**non è permesso ...**
not drinking water	**acqua non potabile**

Insight

Italian is unusual in that a double negative doesn't make a positive, but reinforces the negative.

• In Italian, **Non ho niente**, which literally means *I haven't got nothing*, actually has the meaning of *I haven't got anything*.

Similarly, **Non c'è nessuno**, literally *There isn't no one*, means *There isn't anyone*.

Interrogative – asking questions

In English we sometimes ask questions by reversing the subject (person) and verb, so that, for example, the statement 'He is in a meeting' becomes 'Is he in a meeting?' as a question. In Italian this is not practical, because the subject pronoun is not usually used. In spoken Italian, the rise and fall of the voice (intonation) shows whether a question or a statement is intended – the voice rises at the end of a question, falls at the end of a statement. As a result, an ordinary sentence and a question can have the same words in the same order. Thus:

Do you speak English?	**Parli inglese?**
You speak English	**Parli inglese.**
You like apples.	**Ti piacciono le mele.**
Do you like apples?	**Ti piacciono le mele?**

Here are some more examples of questions; the normal answer expected would begin with sì or no:

Did you go to town?	**Sei andato in città?**
Have you seen him?	**Lo hai visto?**
Did you try the steak?	**Hai assaggiato la bistecca?**
Have you seen the film?	**Hai visto il film?**

Can you drive a car?	**Sai guidare la macchina?**
Do you smoke?	**Lei fuma?**
Do you prefer red or white wine?	**Preferisce vino rosso o bianco?**
Do you eat fish?	**Mangia pesce?**
Are you taking medication?	**Lei prende medicinali?**

There are several words which can introduce a question, as you can see in the following examples:

Who *opened the door?*	**Chi** ha aperto la porta?
What *do you want?*	**Che** vuoi?
What *have you got in your pocket?*	**Che cosa** hai in tasca?
What *do you want to eat?*	**Cosa** volete da mangiare?
What *is her name?*	**Come** si chiama lei?
Why *are you doing that?*	**Perché** fai questo?
What *do you want it **for**?*	**Perché** lo vuoi?
Where *is your girlfriend?*	**Dov'è** la tua amica?
Which *book do you want?*	**Quale** libro vuoi?
Which ones *would you like?*	**Quali** volete?
When *will the train arrive?*	**Quando** arriverà il treno?
How much *money do you need?*	Di **quanti** soldi hai bisogno?
How many *apples do you want?*	**Quante** mele vuole?
How long *have you been here?*	**Da quanto tempo** sei qui?

Remember that you need to consider whether you are addressing the other person formally (**Lei**) or informally (**tu**) as this will affect the form of the verb.

Adverbs

You will remember that adjectives add information about nouns. In the same way, the main use of adverbs is to add information about actions. Many useful adverbs are based on adjectives. Just as in English we add *-ly* to the adjective, Italian adds **-mente** to the feminine form (if there is one – otherwise use the masculine). There are a few adverbs which don't follow this pattern: they are given first in the following table of useful adverbs.

adjective	meaning	adverb	meaning
		molto	very
		abbastanza	quite
buono	good	bene	well
cattivo	bad	male	badly
precedente	previous	prima	previously
veloce	quick, fast, rapid	velocemente	quickly, fast, rapidly
lento	slow	lentamente	slowly
immediato	immediate	immediata-mente	immediately
completo	complete	completa-mente	completely
improvviso	sudden	improvvisa-mente	suddenly
silenzioso	noiseless	silenziosa-mente	noiselessly
conveniente	convenient	conveniente-mente	conveniently
tecnico	technical	tecnicamente	technically
triste	sad	tristemente	sadly
frequente	frequent	frequente-mente	frequently
raro	rare	raramente	rarely
prossimo	next	prossima-mente	soon

Here are some additional adverbs and adverbial phrases, which do not fit into any pattern:

ogni tanto	*occasionally*
qualche volta	*sometimes*
spesso	*often*
molto spesso	*very often*
adesso	*now*
già	*already*
presto	*soon*
prima	*before*
dopo	*afterwards*
poi	*then*
un poco	*a little*

Just like adjectives, adverbs can also have comparative and superlative forms. They are formed in the same way, as shown in the first two examples in the following table; note also the special forms based on **bene** and **male**.

adverb	comparative	superlative
velocemente	più velocemente	il più velocemente (possibile)
fast	*faster*	*fastest*
lentamente	più lentamente	il più lentamente (possibile)
slowly	*slower*	*slowest*
bene	meglio	il meglio (possibile)
well	*better*	*best*
male	peggio	il peggio (possibile)
badly	*worse*	*worst*

Colours and sizes

Colours I colori

Here is a list of common colours. Remember, these are all adjectives, so they go after the noun and follow the usual rules of agreement with nouns. To remind you, those ending in -o also have endings in -a, -i and -e; those ending in -e just have a plural ending in -i. There are also three which are invariable, marked (inv.), which don't change at all.

black	**nero**
blue	**azzurro / blu (inv.)**
brown	**marrone**
green	**verde**
grey	**grigio**
mauve	**malva** (inv.)
orange	**arancione**
pink	**rosa** (inv.)
purple	**viola** (inv.)
red	**rosso**
white	**bianco**
yellow	**giallo**

Here are examples of colours in use:

a red car	**una macchina rossa**
a black suit	**un abito nero**
a pink jumper	**un maglione rosa**
a pink blouse	**una camicetta rosa**
a blue shirt	**una camicia azzurra**
blue trainers	**scarpe da ginnastica azzurre/blu**
grey shoes	**scarpe grigie**
brown gloves	**guanti marroni**

Finally, here is a list of most of the other colours you are likely to need.

blue-grey	**grigiazzurro**
light / pale blue	**azzurro chiaro / celeste**
dark blue	**azzurro scuro / blu (inv.)**
cream / ivory	**color crema (inv.)**
salmon pink	**rosa salmone (inv.)**
fuchsia	**fucsia (inv.)**
khaki	**cachi (inv.)**
burgundy	**granata (inv.)**
lilac	**lilla (inv.)**
navy blue	**blu scuro**
royal blue	**azzurro reale**
pale green	**verde chiaro**
dark green	**verde scuro**
olive green	**verde oliva (inv.)**
bright red	**rosso acceso**
scarlet	**scarlatto**
beige	**beige (inv.)**
emerald	**verde smeraldo**
ruby	**(color) rubino (inv.)**
sapphire	**blu zaffiro (inv.)**
turquoise	**(color) turchese (inv.)**

Sizes **Le misure e le taglie**

Sizes too are adjectives, and follow the normal rules on position and agreement.

very small	**molto piccolo**
small	**piccolo**
medium	**medio**
average	**medio**
large	**grande**
very large	**molto grande**
wide	**largo**
narrow	**stretto**

long	**lungo**	
short (objects)	**corto**	
short (people)	**basso / piccolo**	

Numbers, days, dates and times

Cardinal numbers **I numeri cardinali**

1 uno/una	13 tredici	25 venticinque
2 due	14 quattordici	26 ventisei
3 tre	15 quindici	27 ventisette
4 quattro	16 sedici	28 ventotto
5 cinque	17 diciassette	29 ventinove
6 sei	18 diciotto	30 trenta
7 sette	19 diciannove	31 trentuno/a
8 otto	20 venti	40 quaranta
9 nove	21 ventuno/a	50 cinquanta
10 dieci	22 ventidue	60 sessanta
11 undici	23 ventitré	70 settanta
12 dodici	24 ventiquattro	80 ottanta

90	novanta	1,000	mille
100	cento	2,000	duemila
101	centouno	2,100	duemilacento
102	centodue	5,000	cinquemila
110	centodieci	10,000	diecimila
150	centocinquanta	million	un milione
200	duecento	billion	un miliardo
300	trecento		
400	quattrocento		
500	cinquecento		

- Numbers written as figures are just as in English, except that 7 is always crossed 7.
- When saying a long number aloud, such as a telephone number, Italians either say each number individually or split the numbers

into pairs, as in this example; note that if there is an odd number, the first three may be expressed as hundreds.

9865423 = nove-otto-sei-cinque-quattro-due-tre
or novecentoottantasei, cinquantaquattro, ventitré

- In Italian usage, as in most other European countries, a full stop is used to indicate thousands instead of a comma, and a comma is used where we use a decimal point.

tremiladuecentoquindici = 3.215
sedici virgola quattro = 16,4

Ordinal numbers I numeri ordinali

These are adjectives ... so remember the rules!

first	**primo**
second	**secondo**
third	**terzo**
fourth	**quarto**
fifth	**quinto**
sixth	**sesto**
seventh	**settimo**
eighth	**ottavo**
ninth	**nono**
tenth	**decimo**
21st	**ventunesimo**
21st birthday	**il ventunesimo compleanno**

Here are some fractions.

half	**la metà**
third	**il terzo**
quarter	**il quarto**
fifth	**il quinto**

Insight

Italian numbers, like German ones, are written as one word when they reach the hundreds and thousands. This means they look daunting, but they aren't – as long as you remember to break them up!

3,624: **tremilaseicentoventiquattro (tre-mila-sei-cento-venti-quattro)**

Don't forget that Italian ordinal numbers (*first*, *second*, etc.) are adjectives, so they have to agree with the nouns they are with:

la prima colazione *breakfast*

Years and centuries **Gli anni e i secoli**

the century	**il secolo**
the 1500s	**il Cinquecento**
the 1900s	**il Novecento, il ventesimo secolo**
the 20th century	**il ventesimo secolo**
the 21st century	**il ventunesimo secolo**
the 22nd century	**il ventiduesimo secolo**
the millennium	**il millennio**
the 1990s	**gli anni novanta**
the year 2000	**l'anno duemila**
the year 2010	**l'anno duemiladieci**
next year	**l'anno prossimo**
last year	**l'anno scorso**
the year before last	**due anni fa**
the year after next	**fra due anni**

Days and months **I giorni e i mesi**

In Italian, days of the week and months of the year are written with a small letter, except when they start a sentence. They are all masculine except **la domenica**.

Monday	**lunedì**	Saturday	**sabato**
Tuesday	**martedì**	Sunday	**domenica**
Wednesday	**mercoledì**	on Thursday	**giovedì**
Thursday	**giovedì**	on Saturdays	**il sabato**
Friday	**venerdì**		
January	**gennaio**	July	**luglio**
February	**febbraio**	August	**agosto**
March	**marzo**	September	**settembre**
April	**aprile**	October	**ottobre**
May	**maggio**	November	**novembre**
June	**giugno**	December	**dicembre**

Expressions of time **Espressioni di tempo**

day	**il giorno**
week	**la settimana**
month	**il mese**
year	**l'anno**
last year / month	**l'anno / il mese scorso**
last week	**la settimana scorsa**
next week	**la settimana prossima**
next month / year	**il mese / l'anno prossimo**
yesterday	**ieri**
the day before yesterday	**l'altro ieri**
today	**oggi**
tomorrow	**domani**
the day after tomorrow	**dopodomani**
early morning	**al mattino presto**
morning	**la mattina**
afternoon	**il pomeriggio**
evening	**la sera**
night	**la notte**
tomorrow morning	**domani mattina**
yesterday afternoon	**ieri pomeriggio**
this afternoon	**questo pomeriggio**
tonight	**stasera**

Dates **Le date**

2nd April	**il due aprile**
31st July	**il trentun luglio**
1st December	**il primo dicembre**
8th February	**l'otto febbraio**

To express dates in Italian, use the masculine article followed by the cardinal number, and then the month. Use the ordinal number only for the first day of the month, e.g. **il primo giugno**. When mentioning the day of the week in the date, Italian drops the article, e.g. **lunedì otto maggio**.

The seasons **Le stagioni**

spring	**la primavera**
summer	**l'estate**
autumn	**l'autunno**
winter	**l'inverno**

The clock **L'orologio**

What time is it?	**Che ora è? / Che ore sono?**
midday / midnight	**è mezzogiorno / mezzanotte**
1 o'clock	**è l'una**
2 o'clock	**sono le due**
3.05	**sono le tre e cinque**
4.10	**sono le quattro e dieci**
5.15	**sono le cinque e un quarto**
6.20	**sono le sei e venti**
7.25	**sono le sette e venticinque**
8.30	**sono le otto e mezzo / mezza**
9.35	**sono le dieci meno venticinque**
10.40	**sono le undici meno venti**
11.45	**sono le dodici meno un quarto**
12.50	**è l'una meno dieci**
13.55	**sono le due meno cinque**

You can see that Italian uses è before 1 o'clock, midday and midnight, which is quite logical since all are singular, then **sono le** for the rest, which are plural. You will also by now have worked out that from the hour to half past, you simply add e and the number, **un quart**o or **mezzo/a,** and then use **meno** from half past up to the hour, calculating backwards from the next hour as in English. You can also add **di/della mattina, di/del pomeriggio, di sera** and **di notte** if you want to be precise, such as in the example:

It is four o'clock in the afternoon.   **Sono le quattro di pomeriggio.**

The 24-hour clock is also used very widely in Italy, especially on the radio and for transport. In these instances the times are expressed pretty much as in English:

It is 0900 hours.	**Sono le ore zero nove.**
It is 1315.	**Sono le tredici e quindici.**
It is 2245.	**Sono le ventidue e quarantacinque.**

Finally, some extra vocabulary and expressions to do with time:

second	**il secondo**
minute	**il minuto**
hour	**l'ora**
half hour	**la mezz'ora**
clock, watch	**l'orologio**
alarm clock	**la sveglia**
early	**presto**
late	**tardi**
sooner or later	**prima o poi**
Better late than never!	**Meglio tardi che mai!**
telling the time	**dire l'ora**
my watch has stopped	**si è fermato il mio orologio**
is (... minutes) fast	**va avanti (di ... minuti)**
is (... minutes) slow	**è indietro di ... minuti**
sunset	**il tramonto**

sunrise	**lo spuntar del sole**
dawn / daybreak	**l'alba**
dusk / nightfall	**il crepuscolo**

Quantity

weight	**il peso**
height	**l'altezza / la statura**
length	**la lunghezza**
size	**la taglia / la misura**

Weights and measures **Pesi e misure**

kilo	**il chilo**
half a kilo	**il mezzo chilo**
500 grammes	**cinquecento grammi / mezzo chilo**
a pound	**una libbra**
a litre	**un litro**
a metre	**un metro**
a centimetre	**un centimetro**
a kilometre	**un chilometro**
a pair	**un paio**
a dozen	**una dozzina**
bottle	**una bottiglia**
jar	**un vasetto**
tin	**una scatola / lattina**
box	**una scatola**
pot	**un vasetto**
package	**un pacco**

lots of (e.g. sugar)	**molto (zucchero)**
lots of (e.g. meat)	**molta (carne)**
lots of (e.g. lemons)	**molti (limoni)**
lots of (e.g. apples)	**molte (mele)**
a little ...	**un poco di ... / un po' di**
a few ...	**alcuni/e ...**
more of	**più di ...**
a portion of	**una porzione di**
about 10	**una decina**
about 15	**una quindicina**
about 20	**una ventina**
about 100	**un centinaio**
about 1000	**un migliaio**

Exclamations, giving orders, being polite

How to say *Please* **and** *Thank you*

Thank you	**Grazie**
Please	**Per favore / per piacere / per cortesia**

You will find that Italians say *don't mention it* far more often than we do: **prego!**

Giving orders/commands

You will remember that Italian has four ways of saying *you*: familiar singular (**tu**), polite singular (**Lei**), plural (**voi**) and 'extra-polite' plural (**Loro**). Look back to *Verbs – infinitives and present tense* in the **Toolbox** to remind yourself when to use each form. In general, when giving orders to strangers you should use the formal or polite form.

Help!	**Aiuto!**
Fire!	**Al fuoco!**

Cheers! (with drink)	**Salute! / Cin, cin!**
Cheers! (thanks)	**Grazie**
Cheers (Goodbye)	**Ciao**
Cheerio	**Ciao**
Please	**Per favore / per piacere / per cortesia**
Wait!	**Aspetta! / Aspetti!**
Stop!	**Fermati! / Si fermi!**
Listen!	**Ascolta! / Ascolti!**
Look!	**Guarda! / Guardi!**
Pass me a knife	**Dammi / Mi dia un coltello**
Fetch a glass	**Portami / Mi porti un bicchiere**
Take the chocolates	**Prendi / Prenda i cioccolatini**
Bring me my bag	**Portami / Mi porti la mia borsa**
Excuse me (listen to me)	**Senti / Senta**
Excuse me (sorry)	**Scusami / (Mi) scusi**
Excuse me (I want to pass)	**Permesso**
I'm sorry	**Scusami / Mi scusi**
I didn't mean it	**Non intendevo farlo**
I didn't know	**Non lo sapevo**
I didn't understand	**Non capivo**
Sorry I'm late	**Scusami / Mi scusi per il ritardo**

Being polite

Yes, please	**Sì, grazie**
No, thank you	**No, grazie**
Don't mention it	**Prego**
Not at all	**Prego**
Pardon? (please repeat)	**Come?**
I didn't catch what you said	**Non ho afferrato bene quello che ha detto**
I don't understand	**Non capisco / Non ho capito**
Can I help you ?	**Desidera?**
Can you help me?	**Mi può aiutare?**
Can you say it again?	**Può ripetere, per favore?**
Can you speak more slowly,	**Parli più lentamente, per favore.**
Please will you write it down?	**Per favore, lo metta per iscritto.**

Italian spelling quirks

This section helps you with the 'spelling quirks' of Italian, and the peculiarities of Italian punctuation. First a few general points:

- Almost all Italian words end in vowels; a handful of consonants occur at the end of words, but relatively rarely. Italian does not like complicated combinations of consonants and often goes for simplified spellings compared to other languages; however, double consonants (two of the same) are common.
- In Italian accents are only ever put on a final vowel: they do not alter the sound of the letter that carries one, but the syllable in which it occurs is pronounced more loudly than the rest of the word.
- As you have seen above in 'Years and centuries' and 'Days and months', Italian uses capital letters less than English, notably not on names of days and months, nationalities and names of languages.
- Punctuation is mostly the same as in English, except as related to numbers (see 'Numbers, days, dates, times').
- Italian intonation has quite a 'sing-song' nature anyway, but remember that in a question the voice rises towards the end, whilst in a normal statement, it rises before a comma, but falls at a colon, semi-colon or full stop. In an exclamation, the most important words are spoken with more emphasis.

Recognizing Italian words

- Modern Italian is derived from the Latin spoken by ordinary Romans. Much vocabulary in English also comes from Latin, either via Norman French, from other Romance languages, or directly from Latin in more recent times (largely in the fields of science or culture). Hence, Italian and English have a lot of vocabulary in common, and many words new to you in Italian will be recognizable via English or any other Romance language you happen to know.

- Italian has also imported words from many other languages over the centuries, including a lot from English, especially in recent years (e.g. *design*, *gadget*, *computer*), mostly in the fields of sport, pop music, business, science and computing. Some imported words keep more or less their original spelling, only sometimes with Italian pronunciation: this is usually the case with words adopted in written form, e.g. *design*. Words imported through spoken language tend to adapt to keep the pronunciation similar: such is the case with **gol, scuter**. Sometimes Italian even 're-invents' an English word, such as **footing**, which we would not use in English to mean *jogging*. It is worth noting that verbs based on imported words tend to be in the **-are** verb family, e.g. **filmare, fotocopiare**.
- New words should not always send you rushing for a dictionary. Often, you will be able to work out the likely meaning from experience, especially if you already know the base word at the core of the new word, or recognize it through English or another language you know. (But beware of **'falsi amici'**, which look the same but are not!) The next two sections will help you to make informed guesses.

Cognates

Cognates are words which come from a common source, and so the meaning of the Italian version should be easy to guess; they can usefully be categorized as follows:

- English words absorbed into Italian without change of meaning:
  shopping, design, marketing, scuter, gol
  Some, like the last two, have spellings 'adapted' into Italian to 'sound' as in English.
- Italian words with common equivalent in English, or English words borrowed from Italian:
  pasta, vino, allegro, concerto
- Words identical in form to their English equivalent and with comparable pronunciation:
  panorama, idea

- Words similar in form to their English equivalent and with comparable pronunciation:
  documento, militare, sistema, clima, movimento, originale
- Verbs whose stem is identical or similar in form to the English equivalent:
  ammirare, contenere, consistere
- Words containing certain frequently occurring Italian orthographic features which, once known, allow ready identification with English equivalents:
  libertà, turismo, indicazione, potenza

Note the equivalent English – Italian suffixes:

-tà = *-ty*	**città** *city*; **capacità** *capacity*
-zione = *-tion*	**azione** *action*; **elezione** *election*
-ia = *-y*	**energia** *energy*; **farmacia** *pharmacy*

Many other prefixes and suffixes can be added to this list.

Derivatives

In both written and spoken Italian, 'undressing' a new word to get at its core often makes it recognizable. It helps to bear in mind plural forms of nouns, adjectival agreement and verb forms, and the basic principles by which these are used. Here are some basic categories of derivative:

- Words whose meaning is determined by common prefixes or suffixes, but with a known or identifiable base form:
  con-: contenere, conseguenza
  s-: sfortuna, snazionalizzare
  dis-: dissuadere, dispensare
  in-/im-: incorrotto, impossibile
  re-/ri-: reversibile, ricominciare
  sub-: subaffittare, subcosciente
  -abile: nota → notabile
  -eria: pasta → pasticceria
  -mento: inquinare → inquinamento
  -oso: arena → arenoso, noia → noioso

- Nouns denoting people and other related concepts, which are characterized by endings such as **-aio/a, -ore/rice, -ista, -eria:**
  - **-aio/-aia:** tabaccaio
  - **-ista:** pianista, tassista
  - **-ore/-rice:** pittore / pittrice, attore / attrice
  - **-eria:** pizzeria, salumeria

  These are mostly based on another noun or a verb.

- Adverbs formed by adding the ending **-mente** to known or easily identifiable adjectives:
  - totalmente, attivamente

  Most adverbs end in **-mente**, just as in English most end in *-ly*.

- Adjectives with ending **-abile** or **-ibile** which compare with English equivalents ending in *-able* or *-ible* deriving from easily known or identifiable words:
  - immaginabile, ammirabile

- Adjectives with ending **-oso/-osa** comparable with English equivalents ending in *-ous*, and which are easily identifiable:
  - religioso, furioso, vigoroso, vizioso

- Adjectives with ending **-ese, -ino/a, -ano/a** comparing with English *-ese* or *-(i)an*, usually indicating place of origin:
  - inglese, giapponese, canadese, fiorentino, napoletano

- Diminutives such as words ending in **-etto/a, -ino/a** deriving from known or other easily identifiable words.
  - signorino, panino, bellino, fioretta

- Augmentative and pejorative suffixes such as **-one/ona, -azzo, -accio/uccio:**
  - filmaccio, erroraccio, cenone

- Compound nouns, consisting of combinations of known words; these often consist of verb and plural form of the noun object of the action implied:
  - apriscatole, portacenere, lavastoviglie

- Words derived from adjectives:
    tranquillizzare, pulizia

- Words mainly derived from verbs, with endings **-ante** or **-ente**:
    cantante, agente

- Place names with identical or similar spelling to English equivalent:
    Italia, America, Brasile

- Common acronyms and initials (often in a different order):

OTAN – Organizzazione del Trattato Nord Atlantico	*NATO*
ONU – Organizzazzione delle Nazioni Unite	*UN – United Nations*
UE – Unione Europea	*EU – European Union*

1

Personal matters

1.1 Titles, greetings and making arrangements

Core vocabulary

Titles **Titoli**

Mr	**signor (Sig.)**
Mrs	**signora (Sig.ra)**
Miss	**signorina (Sig.rina)**
Sir	**Signore**
Madam	**Signora**

Signore is used for both *Mr* and *Sir*; the latter is used to a stranger by, for example, a shop assistant, and by a serviceman to a senior officer; **signora** is used for both *Mrs* and *Madam* in the same way, and **signorina** is always used for *Miss*. All of these are used with the person's surname, whether or not their first name is also being used, and are preceded with **il** or **la** except when you are speaking direct to *him / her*:

> il signor Bianchi; la signora Colombo;
> 'Buongiorno signorina Borelli'.

Italian people usually use **dottor(e)** when referring to or addressing

a doctor, even though the normal word for the profession is
medico. They also address as **dottor(e)** anybody who has graduated
from university and any person in a senior position. A lawyer is
referred to as **avvocato**, teachers can be addressed as **professore**
and engineers are often referred to as **ingegnere**. The abbreviations
used in front of the person's name when written are: **Dott., Avv.,
Prof.**, and **Ing.** The normal word for *boss* is **padrone**.

Greetings **Saluti**

Hello, hi	**Ciao!**
Good morning	**Buongiorno**
Good afternoon, Good evening	**Buona sera**
Good night	**Buona notte**
Goodbye	**Arrivederci / Ciao** (informal)

Note that **sera** is used both for late afternoon and evening, and
lasts from approximately 5 p.m. to midnight. **Buona notte** can be
used only when you are leaving someone late in the evening, to go
home or to bed.

Introducing someone **Presentare qualcuno**

This is ...	**Questo è ...**
May I introduce ...?	**Ti/Le presento ...**
Are you (Mr ...)?	**Lei è ...?**
Do you know (Mr ...)?	**Conosce ...?**
Mr What's-his-name	**il Signor Coso**
Mrs What's-her-name	**la Signora Cosa**
Pleased to meet you	**Piacere (di conoscerla)**
May I sit here?	**Posso sedermi qui?**
Are you alone?	**Lei è solo / sola?**
I am ...	**Sono ... / Mi chiamo ...**
single	**celibe (male) / nubile (female)**
married	**sposato/a**
divorced	**divorziato/a**
separated	**separato/a**
a widow	**vedova**
a widower	**vedovo**

Making arrangements **Organizzare qualcosa**

What shall we do this evening?	**Che cosa facciamo stasera?**
Hello	**Ciao! (familiar) / Buongiorno! (formal)**
May I introduce myself?	**Mi presento**
This is my wife/husband/ friend	**Ti/Le presento mia moglie /mio marito / il mio amico /la mia amica**
Pleased to meet you	**Molto lieto / piacere!**
May I sit here?	**Posso sedermi qui?**
Are you alone?	**Sei solo/a? / Lei è solo/a?**
May I invite you to a ...?	**Vorrei invitarti/La a ...?**
bar	**un bar**
night club	**un night(club)**
restaurant	**un ristorante**
theatre	**un teatro**
cinema	**un cinema**
dance	**un ballo**
drink	**prendere qualche cosa**
meal / lunch / dinner	**mangiare / pranzo / cena**
dance	**ballare**
show	**uno spettacolo**
play	**un'opera teatrale**
musical	**un musical**
comedy	**una commedia**
concert	**un concerto**

Useful verbs

to introduce	**presentare**
to arrange a meeting	**fissare un appuntamento**
to book a table	**riservare un tavolo**
to go to the cinema	**andare al cinema**
to go to the theatre	**andare al teatro**
to go out	**uscire**
to go to a night club	**andare in un night (club)**
to watch a video	**vedere un video**

Useful phrases

How are you?	**Come stai? / Come sta?**
How's it going?	**Come va?**
Very well thank you	**Molto bene, grazie**
Have a nice day / weekend	**Buona giornata / Buon fine settimana**
See you soon	**A presto**
See you later	**A più tardi**
See you next time	**Alla prossima volta**
See you tomorrow	**A domani**
What would you like to do?	**Che ti/le piacerebbe fare?**
Where would you like to go?	**Dove ti/Le piacerebbe andare?**
When shall we meet?	**A che ora ci ritroviamo?**
I will pick you up	**Passerò a prenderti/la**
Excuse me	**Scusa (familiar) / Scusi (formal)**
Pardon?	**Come? / Scusi? / Prego?**
I don't understand	**Non capisco**
Can you speak more slowly	**Parla / Parli più lentamente**
I apologize / I'm sorry	**Mi scusi**
I beg your pardon	**Prego**
I didn't mean it	**Non avevo l'intenzione di farlo**
Forgive me	**Scusami (familiar) / Mi scusi (formal)**
... it was my fault	**è stata colpa mia**
It was your fault	**È stata colpa tua / Sua**
Thank you very much	**Grazie mille**
I enjoyed it very much	**Mi è piaciuto molto**
I had a lovely time	**Mi sono divertito molto**
We must do it again sometime	**Dobbiamo farlo un'altra volta**
I will see you tomorrow / later	**Ci vediamo domani / più tardi**
I would like to see you again	**Mi piacerebbe vederti/la un'altra volta**

It's a pleasure	**È un piacere / Prego!**
Have a good time!	**Buon divertimento!**
Have a safe journey	**Buon viaggio**
Good luck	**Buona fortuna!**
All the best	**Che tutto vada per il meglio!**
Happy birthday	**Buon compleanno**
Merry Christmas	**Buon Natale**
Congratulations	**Congratulazioni**
Happy New Year	**Buon Anno**
Anyway ...	**In ogni caso ... / comunque ...**
Er ...	**Ehm ...**
Uhm ...	**Mmm ...**
Ah!	**Aaa!**
etc. (etcetera)	**ecc. (eccetera)**
i.e. (that is)	**cioè**
e.g. (for example)	**ad es. (ad esempio)**
a.s.a.p (as soon as possible)	**prima possibile**

How to say *you*

Dare del tu / dare del Lei

In Italian, you need to decide how to address the person you are
speaking to. The informal **tu** is used for family, close friends and
acquaintances, and in most cases anyone of an age and status
similar to yours, even if you don't yet know them. The formal **Lei**
is used for strangers and those older than you or senior in status.
In Italy this is more relaxed than it used to be, but if in doubt when
meeting someone for the first time, use **Lei** until invited to use **tu**.
Your new acquaintance will probably use an expression such as
'**mi potresti dare del tu**' to invite you to be informal. Just to remind
you, where both **tu** and **Lei** forms of a verb are given, the **tu** form
is first.

English has no 'familiar' and 'polite' forms of *you* (it used to have the familiar *thou* and the polite *you*, but *thou* has fallen into disuse). Italian, however, uses **Lei**, which is the word for *she* with a capital letter. This is because a way of according people respect used to be not to address them directly, but to use the third person. This contrasts with French (where respect was accorded by addressing someone in the plural) and German (where respect was accorded by addressing people in the plural *and* the third person!).

1.2 Where are you from?

Core vocabulary

Where do you come from? **Di dove sei? / Di dov'è?**

I come from ...	**Sono di**
I am ...	**Sono ...**
I speak ...	**Parlo ...**

Austria	**Austria**	*Austrian*	**austriaco/a**
Belgium	**Belgio**	*Belgian*	**belga**
Ireland	**Irlanda**	*Irish*	**irlandese**
England	**Inghilterra**	*English*	**inglese**
France	**Francia**	*French*	**francese**
Germany	**Germania**	*German*	**tedesco/a**
Greece	**Grecia**	*Greek*	**greco/a**
Italy	**Italia**	*Italian*	**italiano/a**
Scotland	**Scozia**	*Scottish*	**scozzese**
Spain	**Spagna**	*Spanish*	**spagnolo/a**
Switzerland	**Svizzera**	*Swiss*	**svizzero/a**
Wales	**Galles**	*Welsh*	**gallese**

In each case the masculine form of the nationality is the name of the language, except in the case of countries which do not have their own language.

Africa	**Africa**	African	**africano/a**
America	**America**	American	**americano/a**
Australia	**Australia**	Australian	**australiano/a**
Croatia	**Croazia**	Croatian	**croato/a**
Denmark	**Danimarca**	Danish	**danese**
Finland	**Finlandia**	Finnish	**finlandese**
Hungary	**Ungheria**	Hungarian	**ungherese**
India	**indiano**	India	**indiano/a**
New Zealand	**Nuova Zelanda**	New Zealander	**neozelandese**
Norway	**Norvegia**	Norwegian	**norvegese**
Poland	**Polonia**	Polish	**polacco/a**
Russia	**Russia**	Russian	**russo/a**
Sweden	**Svezia**	Swedish	**svedese**

There are a number of British place names for which there is an Italian version:

the United Kingdom	**Il Regno Unito**
Great Britain	**Gran Bretagna**
England	**Inghilterra**
Wales	**Galles**
Scotland	**Scozia**
Northern Ireland	**Irlanda del Nord**
London	**Londra**
Edinburgh	**Edimburgo**
Thames	**Il Tamigi**
Cornwall	**Cornovaglia**

There are also a number of foreign cities which have an Italian version:

Athens	**Atene**
Belgrade	**Belgrado**
Moscow	**Mosca**
Paris	**Parigi**
Berlin	**Berlino**
Stockholm	**Stoccolma**
Hamburg	**Amburgo**
the Hague	**L'Aia**

Useful phrases

Do you speak English?	**Parli inglese? / Parla inglese?**
What languages do you speak?	**Che lingue parli / parla?**
What nationality are you?	**Di che nazionalità sei / è?**
Where were you born?	**Dove sei nato/a? / Dov'è nato/a?**
I was born in ...	**Sono nato/a in ...**
I live ...	**Vivo / Abito ...**
in the north / south / east / west	**nel nord / nel sud / nell'est / nell'ovest**
in the middle	**nel centro**
near the sea	**vicino al mare**
on the coast	**sulla costa**
in the mountains	**in montagna**
in the city	**in città**
in a village	**in un paese / villaggio**
in the suburbs	**in periferia**
in the country	**in campagna**

Useful verbs

to live	**vivere / abitare**	*I live ...*	**vivo / abito**
to speak	**parlare**	*I speak*	**parlo**
to be born	**nascere**	*I was born in ...*	**sono nato/a in ...**

1.3 Personal appearance

Core vocabulary

What are you like?	**Come sei / Com'è?**
I am a ...	**Sono un(a) ...**
What does he/she look like?	**Com'è lui/lei?**
He / She is a ...	**È ...**
man	**un uomo**
woman	**una donna**

girl	**una ragazza**		
boy	**un ragazzo**		
teenager	**un/un'adolescente**		
child	**un bambino / una bambina**		
baby	**un bambino piccolo / una bambina piccola**		

Use the following grid to help you to build up what you need to be able to say to describe yourself and someone you know well.

I am	**Sono**	*quite* **abbastanza**	*tall* **alto/a**
Are you ...?	**È / Sei ...?**	*very* **molto**	*short/small* **piccolo/a** **basso/a**
He/She is	**Lui/lei è**	*average*	*di statura* **media**

I have	**Ho**	*long blonde hair* **capelli biondi lunghi**
He has	**(Lui) ha**	*short brown hair* **capelli castani corti**
She has	**(Lei) ha**	*medium length dark hair* **capelli scuri di media lunghezza**
I have	**Ho**	*blue/brown eyes* **occhi azzurri/castani**

attractive	**attraente**	*unattractive*	**poco attraente**
fashionable	**di moda**	*unfashionable*	**fuori moda**
fit	**in forma**	*unfit*	**non in forma**
good looking	**bello/a**	*ugly*	**brutto/a**
neat	**ordinato/a**	*untidy*	**disordinato/a**
smart	**elegante**	*scruffy*	**trasandato/a**
ordinary	**normale**	*different*	**diverso**

tall	**alto/a**	*short*	**basso/a**
underweight	**sottopeso/a**	*overweight*	**sovrappeso/a**
well built	**ben fatto**	*weak/skinny*	**debole / magro/a**
anorexic	**anoressico/a**	*obese*	**obeso/a**
right-handed	**che usa la mano destra**	*left-handed*	**mancino/a**
short-sighted	**miope**	*long sighted*	**presbite**
agoraphobic	**agorafobo/a**	*claustrophobic*	**claustrofobico/a**

Here are some of the more colloquial words used in Italy to describe people:

butch (man)	**macho**
butch (woman)	**mascolina**
getting on a bit	**di una certa età**
teenager	**l'adolescente**
brat, kid, youngster	**moccioso/a**
bird (girl)	**la tipa/bambola**
cool, handsome	**figo**

Useful phrases

How much do you weigh?	**Quanto pesi? / Quanto pesa?**
I weigh 75 kg	**Peso 75 kg**
How tall are you?	**Quanto sei alto/a? / Quanto è alto/a?**
I am 1.59 m	**Sono alto/a 1.59 m**

Useful verbs

to look like someone	**rassomigliare a qualcuno**
to put on weight	**ingrassare**
to lose weight	**dimagrire**
to get fit	**mettersi in forma**

1.4 What sort of person are you?

Core vocabulary

Character and feelings **Temperamento e sentimenti**
If you are describing somebody, you need to decide whether
you are talking about their character, in which case you need an
expression with the verb **essere** like those in the following chart, or
you are talking about how they are or how they feel, in which case
you need an expression with the verb **stare**. Remember that the
adjectives have to agree with the noun.

I am	sono	*shy / talkative*	timido / loquace
are you?	sei / è?	*happy / unhappy*	felice / infelice
he is	(lui) è	*friendly / unfriendly*	amichevole / poco amichevole
she is	(lei) è	*nice / nasty*	simpatico / antipatico

I am	sono	*happy / sad*	contento / triste
are you?	sei / è?	*awake / tired*	sveglio / stanco
he is	(lui) è	*smart / scruffy*	elegante / trasandato
she is	(lei) è	*in a good / bad mood*	di buon / cattivo umore

Here are some extra adjectives you could use to describe people.

good	**buono**	bad	**cattivo**
hard-working	**diligente**	*lazy*	**pigro**
interesting	**interessante**	*boring*	**noioso**
quiet	**tranquillo**	*loud*	**rumoroso**
strong	**forte**	*weak*	**debole**

capable	**capace**	*useless*	**incapace**
confident	**sicuro di sé**	*nervous*	**nervoso/ansioso**
generous	**generoso**	*mean*	**tirchio**
helpful	**disponibile**	*unhelpful*	**poco disponibile**
odd	**strano**	*normal*	**normale**
polite	**educato**	*rude*	**maleducato**
practical	**pratico**	*impractical*	**poco pratico**
reliable	**affidabile**	*unreliable*	**inaffidabile**
relaxed	**rilassato**	*up-tight*	**teso**
sensible	**sensato**	*stupid*	**stupido**
sensitive	**sensibile**	*unfeeling*	**insensibile**
serious	**serio**	*frivolous*	**frivolo**
sincere	**sincero**	*insincere*	**insincero**
strong-willed	**prepotente**	*weak*	**debole**
well-behaved	**che si comporta bene**	*badly behaved*	**che si comporta male**
up-to-date	**di moda**	*out-of-date*	**fuori moda**

The five senses **I cinque sensi**

sight	**la vista**	*to see*	**vedere**	*I see*	**vedo**
hearing	**l'udito**	*to hear*	**sentire**	*I hear*	**sento**
taste	**il gusto**	*to taste*	**assaggiare**	*I taste*	**assaggio**
smell	**l'olfatto**	*to smell*	**sentire odore di**	*I smell*	**sento odore di**
touch	**il tatto**	*to touch*	**toccare**	*I touch*	**tocco**

Useful phrases

He / she has ...	**(Lui / lei) ha ...**
a sense of humour	**il senso dell'umorismo**
plenty of will power	**molta forza di volontà**
a kind heart	**bontà di cuore**
a weakness for ...	**un debole per ...**
a good imagination	**una buon'immaginazione**

Useful verbs

to get bored	**annoiarsi**
I am getting bored	**mi annoio**
to be interested in something	**interessarsi a/di**
I am interested	**mi interesso a/di**
to be worried about something	**preoccuparsi di**
I am worried	**mi preoccupo di**

Other useful adjectives

angry	**arrabbiato**
annoyed	**seccato**
kind	**gentile**
unkind	**poco gentile**
laid back	**rilassato**
dynamic	**dinamico**

False friends

You may have noticed a couple of **falsi amici** *false friends* in this area. This table should help you:

English	Italian
sensitive	**sensibile**
sensible	**sensato**
nice, kind	**simpatico**
sympathetic	**comprensivo**

Lots of expressions we use in English like *to be hot, cold, hungry, thirsty* and so on are expressed in Italian using the verb **avere** as in the following table:

to be hot	avere caldo	I am hot	ho caldo
to be cold	avere freddo	he is cold	ha freddo
to be hungry	avere fame	we are hungry	abbiamo fame
to be thirsty	avere sete	you are thirsty	hai sete
to be tired	avere sonno	they are tired	hanno sonno
to be in a hurry	avere fretta	she is in a hurry	ha fretta
to be afraid	avere paura	they are afraid	hanno paura

1.5 My things

Core vocabulary

things	le cose
bag	la borsa
briefcase	la cartella
cheque book	il libretto degli assegni
credit cards	le carte di credito
diary	l'agenda
driving licence	la patente di guida
glasses / sunglasses	gli occhiali (da sole)
keys	le chiavi
note book	il taccuino / il bloc-notes
passport	il passaporto
pen	la penna
purse	il portamonete
wallet	il portafoglio
watch	l'orologio

The words for *my/your/his/her/our/their* follow this pattern:

my	il mio, la mia, i miei, le mie
your (familiar)	il tuo, la tua, i tuoi, le tue
his, her, your (formal)	il suo, la sua, i suoi, le sue
our	il nostro, la nostra, i nostri, le nostre
your	il vostro, la vostra, i vostri, le vostre
their, your (formal)	il loro, la loro, i loro, le loro

On my desk **Sulla mia scrivania**

computer	**il computer**
hard drive	**l'hard disk**
mobile	**il telefonino / cellulare**
mouse	**il mouse**
laptop	**il laptop**
palm-top	**il palmare**
PC	**il PC**
phone	**il telefono**
printer	**la stampante**
scanner	**lo scanner**

At home **A casa**

DVD player	**il lettore DVD**
CD player	**il lettore CD**
discs	**i dischi**
camera	**la macchina fotografica**
video camera	**la videocamera**
digital camera	**la macchina fotografica digitale**
film	**la pellicola**
roll of film	**il rullino**
photos	**le foto**

My friends **I miei amici / le mie amiche**

girl friend(s)	**le mie amiche**
boy friend(s)	**i miei amici**
girlfriend	**la mia ragazza**
boyfriend	**il mio ragazzo**
colleagues	**i miei colleghi**

Here are a few expressions used in colloquial Italian:

my bike	**la mia bici**
my TV	**la mia tivù**
my better half	**la mia dolce metà**
my kids	**i miei bambini**

Have you got a … ?	**Hai / Ha un/uno/una/un'…?**
I have lost my …	**Ho perso (perduto) il mio / la mia / i miei / le mie …**
I can't find my …	**Non trovo il mio / la mia / i miei / le mie…**
Have you seen my …?	**Hai / Ha visto il mio / la mia / i miei / le mie…?**

Useful verbs

to lose / mislay	**perdere**
to find	**trovare**
to forget	**dimenticare**

1.6 I think, I feel

Core vocabulary

to like	**piacere**	*I like*	**mi piace**
to love	**amare**	*I love*	**amo**
to prefer	**preferire**	*I prefer*	**preferisco**
to dislike	**non piacere**	*I dislike*	**non mi piace**
to hate	**odiare**	*I hate*	**odio**

The verb **piacere** is used to express the idea of liking, but has to do it back-to-front, because it really means '*to please*'! So what you really say is '*this car pleases me*' '**mi piace questa macchina**'. Study the following table and learn the examples to help you remember how to use this expression. Note how the person word changes, and that only two verb endings are used, to match the thing or things liked, not the person liking. It really is back to front!

	singular things	plural things
I like	mi piace	mi piacciono
you like (familiar sing.)	ti piace	ti piacciono
he / she likes	gli / le piace	gli / le piacciono
you like (formal sing.)	Le piace	Le piacciono
we like	ci piace	ci piacciono
you like (familiar pl.)	vi piace	vi piaccciono
they like	gli piace	gli piacciono
you like (formal pl.)	piace a Loro	piacciono a Loro

I like wine	**mi piace il vino**
I like tomatoes	**mi piacciono i pomodori**
you like beer	**ti piace la birra**
you like oranges	**ti piacciono le arance**
he likes football	**gli piace il calcio**
she likes sweets	**le piacciono le caramelle**
we like Italy	**ci piace l'Italia**
we like Italian people	**ci piacciono gli italiani**
you like working	**vi piace lavorare**
you like public holidays	**vi piacciono i giorni festivi**
they like travelling	**gli piace viaggiare**
they like holidays	**gli piacciono le vacanze**

to believe	**credere**	I believe	**credo**
to think	**pensare**	I think	**penso**
to feel	**sentirsi**	I feel	**mi sento**
to worry	**preoccuparsi**	I worry	**mi preoccupo**
to advise	**consigliare**	I advise	**consiglio**
to encourage	**incoraggiare**	I encourage	**incoraggio**
to exaggerate	**esagerare**	I am exaggerating	**esagero**
to joke	**scherzare**	I am joking	**sto scherzando**
to lie	**dire bugie**	I am lying	**dico bugie**
to promise	**promettere**	I promise	**prometto**

Note that **credere** and **pensare** need a subjunctive verb after them when used in the negative if there is a subordinate clause (See 'Toolbox', under 'Conditionals and subjunctives')

non credo che ci sia	*I don't believe he/she is there*
non penso che abbiano paura	*I don't think they are afraid*

Useful verbs

to be disappointed	**essere deluso**
to be relieved	**essere sollevato**
to be depressed	**essere depresso**
to be elated	**essere euforico**
to be stressed	**essere stressato**
to be relaxed	**essere rilassato**
to be discouraged	**essere scoraggiato**
to be encouraged	**essere incoraggiato**
to be embarrassed	**essere imbarazzato**
to be at ease	**essere/sentirsi a proprio agio**
to be nervous	**essere nervoso**
to be confident	**essere sicuro**
to be worried	**essere preoccupato**
to be reassured	**essere rassicurato**
to be sad	**essere triste**
to be happy	**essere contento**
to be ashamed	**vergognarsi**
to be proud	**essere orgoglioso/fiero**
to be unfortunate	**essere sfortunato**
to be fortunate	**essere fortunato**

Verbs which are used with another verb

to want to	**volere**	*I want to go*	**voglio andare**
to be able to	**potere**	*I can go in*	**posso entrare**
to have to	**dovere**	*I must leave*	**devo partire**
to need to	**avere bisogno di**	*I need to go out*	**ho bisogno di uscire**
ought to / should	**dovere**	*I should stay at home*	**dovrei rimanere a casa**

Useful phrases

There are a number of impersonal expressions in Italian which consist of è + an adjective + an infinitive.

it's necessary	**è necessario arrivare alle dieci**	*it's necessary to arrive at ten*
it's vital	**è essenziale farlo**	*it's vital to do it*
it's obligatory	**è obbligatorio pagare la bolletta**	*it's obligatory to pay the bill*
it's possible	**è possibile uscire**	*it's possible to go out*
it's impossible	**è impossibile sapere**	*it's impossible to know*
it's dangerous	**è pericoloso nuotare qui**	*it's dangerous to swim here*
it's horrible	**è orribile vederlo così**	*it's horrible to see him like this*
it's prohibited	**è vietato attaccare manifesti**	*it's prohibited to put up posters*

What is it like?

acceptable	**accettabile**	*comfortable*	**comodo**
considerable	**considerevole**	*probable*	**probabile**
possible	**possibile**	*preferable*	**preferibile**
remarkable	**straordinario**	*responsible*	**responsabile**
tolerable	**sopportabile**		

Most words which end in *-able* or *-ible* in English are similar in Italian, adding an extra -i before -le, but in Italian remember to pronounce the vowels clearly and to stress the a of -**abile** or the i of -**ibile**.

1.7 Expressing an opinion

to believe	**credere**	I believe	**credo**
to consider	**considerare**	I consider	**considero**
to think	**pensare**	I think	**penso**
to agree / disagree	**essere / non essere d'accordo**	I agree / disagree	**sono / non sono d'accordo**
to argue (maintain)	**sostenere**	I argue	**discuto**
to argue (debate)	**discutere**	I argue	**dibatto**
to ask	**domandare**	I ask	**domando**
to dispute	**contestare**	I dispute	**contesto**
to question	**mettere in dubbio**	I question	**metto in dubbio**
to quote	**citare**	I quote	**cito**
to request	**chiedere**	I request	**chiedo**
to suggest	**suggerire**	I suggest	**suggerisco**
to state	**dichiarare**	I would like to say	**dichiaro**
to compare	**confrontare**	I compare	**confronto**
to contrast	**contrastare**	I contrast	**contrasto**
to differ	**dissentire**	I differ	**dissento**
to discuss	**discutere**	I discuss	**discuto**
to conclude	**concludere**	I conclude	**concludo**

on the one hand	**da una parte**
on the other hand	**d'altra parte**
firstly	**in primo luogo**
secondly	**in secondo luogo**
finally	**alla fine**
actually	**veramente**
basically	**fondamentalmente**
clearly	**chiaramente**
consequently	**di conseguenza / quindi**
fortunately / unfortunately	**fortunatamente / purtroppo**
generally	**generalmente**
honestly	**francamente**
mainly	**principalmente / soprattutto**

normally	**normalmente**
obviously	**ovviamente**
particularly	**specialmente**
principally	**principalmente**
really	**davvero**
usually/unusually	**di solito / insolitamente**
in my / his / her opinion	**secondo me / lui / lei**
above all	**soprattutto**
although	**benché**
as a result	**di conseguenza**
as well as	**oltre a**
however	**però / comunque**
in some respects	**sotto certi aspetti**
in spite of	**malgrado**
instead of	**invece di**
nevertheless	**tuttavia**
otherwise	**altrimenti**
similarly	**allo stesso modo**
the reason is	**è perché**
to tell the truth	**a dire la verità**
I wish I could agree	**vorrei poter essere d'accordo**
I beg to differ	**mi permetto di non essere d'accordo**
I mean	**voglio dire**
I maintain	**sosteng**
for example	**per esempio**
etc.	**eccetera / ecc.**
in brief	**in breve**
the advantages / disadvantages are	**i vantaggi / gli svantaggi sono**
the pros and cons	**i pro e i contro**
to conclude	**concludere**
it is	**è**
bad / good	**cattivo / male / buono / bene**
comfortable / uncomfortable	**comodo / scomodo**
better / worse	**migliore / meglio / peggiore / peggio**
nice / not very nice	**piacevole / spiacevole**
too hard / easy	**troppo difficile / facile**

1.8 *I do* (*I* + useful action verbs)

Useful verbs

to wake up	svegliarsi	I wake up	mi sveglio
to get up	alzarsi	I get up	mi alzo
to take a shower	fare la doccia	I take a shower	faccio la doccia
to get dressed	vestirsi	I get dressed	mi vesto
to eat	mangiare	I eat	mangio
to drink	bere	I drink	bevo
to work	lavorare	I work	lavoro
to go home	tornare a casa	I go home	torno a casa
to play	giocare	I play	gioco
to watch	guardare la televisione	I watch television	guardo la televisione
to read	leggere	I read	leggo
to get washed	lavarsi	I get washed	mi lavo
to go to bed	andare a letto	I go to bed	vado a letto
to laugh	ridere	I laugh	rido
to smile	sorridere	I smile	sorrido
to giggle	avere la risarella	I giggle	ho la risarella
to sleep	dormire	I sleep	dormo
to dream	sognare	I dream	sogno

Coming and going verbs **Verbi di movimento**

to walk	camminare	I walk	cammino
to run	correre	I run	corro
to ride	andare a / in	I ride	vado a / in
to drive	guidare	I drive	guido
to arrive	arrivare	I arrive	arrivo
to depart	partire	I depart	parto
to enter	entrare	I enter	entro
to leave	partire	I leave	parto
to come	venire	I come	vengo
to go	andare	I go	vado

to go up	**salire**	*I go up*	**salgo**
to go down	**scendere**	*I go down*	**scendo**
to stay	**rimanere**	*I stay*	**rimango**
to return	**tornare**	*I return*	**torno**

Communicating **Comunicare**

to speak	**parlare**
to repeat something	**ripetere qualcosa**
to talk to someone	**parlare con qualcuno**
to whisper to someone	**bisbigliare a qualcuno**
to shout at someone	**gridare a qualcuno**
to ask a question	**fare una domanda**
to ask for something	**chiedere qualcosa**
to respond to a question	**rispondere a una domanda**
to tell a story	**raccontare una storia**
to enjoy yourself	**divertirsi**
to get angry	**arrabbiarsi**
to have trouble / difficulty	**avere difficoltà**
to get depressed	**deprimersi**
to know / meet someone	**conoscere / incontrare qualcuno**
to know something	**sapere qualcosa**
to cheat	**imbrogliare**
to trick	**ingannare**
to challenge	**sfidare**
to compliment	**complimentarsi con**
to neglect	**trascurare**

··

Insight

In Italian the infinitive (*to* form) of reflexive verbs (verbs that are used with a pronoun like **mi, ti, si,** etc.) is written with the pronoun on the end. This can look odd, and is quite often encountered on signs and notices (for instance **È pericoloso sporgersi, Munirsi del biglietto**).

··

1.9 Don't panic!

Useful phrases

Help!	**Aiuto!**
Listen!	**Ascolta! / Ascolti!**
Do you understand?	**Capisci? / Capisce?**
Understood?	**Hai capito? / Ha capito?**
Can you help me?	**Mi puoi / può aiutare?**
Do you speak English?	**Parli / Parla inglese?**
Can you speak more slowly?	**Parla / Parli più lentamente!**
I didn't catch what you said	**Non ho colto quello che hai/ ha detto**
Please can you find someone who speaks English?	**Può trovare qualcuno che parli inglese?**
Can you write it down for me please?	**Scrivilo / Lo scriva per favore**
How do you spell it?	**Come si scrive?**
Have you got the phone number for ...?	**Hai / Ha il numero di telefono ...?**
police	**della polizia**
fire brigade	**dei vigili del fuoco**
ambulance	**dell'ambulanza**
doctor	**del medico**
breakdown services	**dei servizi di soccorso stradale**
What do I need to dial first?	**Quale prefisso devo comporre?**
What is the code for ...?	**Qual è il prefisso di/per ...?**
How do I get an outside line?	**Come posso avere una linea esterna?**
Danger	**Pericolo**
Watch out!	**Attenzione!**
Warning	**Avviso**
No entry	**Vietato l'ingresso**

TEST YOURSELF

Unjumble these sentences so that they make sense. Check your answers against the solutions given. And it is a good idea to make sure you understand the meaning of each sentence as well, and didn't just get lucky!

1 mia moglie. presento Ti
2 altra Dobbiamo farlo un' volta.
3 andare? Dove piacerebbe ti
4 Calabria? è il per prefisso Qual Reggio
5 che inglese? parla Può qualcuno trovare
6 è nuotare qui. pericoloso
7 abbiano che Non paura. penso
8 bolletta.è la obbligatorio pagare
9 che sei? Di nazionalità
10 Ci gli Italiani. piacciono

Answers:
1 Ti presento mia moglie
2 Dobbiamo farlo un'altra volta
3 Dove ti piacerebbe andare?
4 Qual è il prefisso per Reggio Calabria?
5 Può trovare qualcuno che parla inglese?
6 È pericoloso nuotare qui
7 Non penso che abbiano paura
8 È obbligatorio pagare la bolletta
9 Di che nazionalità sei?
10 Ci piacciono gli Italiani.

2

....

Family

2.1 My family

Core vocabulary

My family and relatives **La mia famiglia e i miei parenti**

my mother	**mia madre**
my father	**mio padre**
my parents	**i miei genitori**
my sister	**mia sorella**
my brother	**mio fratello**
my younger brother	**il mio fratello minore**
my younger sister	**la mia sorella minore**
my older brother	**il mio fratello maggiore**
my older sister	**la mia sorella maggiore**
my half-brother	**il mio fratellastro**
my half-sister	**la mia sorellastra**
twin brother	**il mio fratello gemello**
twin sister	**la mia sorella gemella**
my grandmother	**mia nonna**
my grandfather	**mio nonno**
my grandparents	**i miei nonni**
my great-grandparents	**i miei bisnonni**
my grandson	**mio nipote**
my granddaughter	**mia nipote**
my uncle	**mio zio**

my aunt	**mia zia**
my cousin (m)	**mio cugino**
my cousin (f)	**mia cugina**
my nephew	**mio nipote**
my niece	**mia nipote**
my husband	**mio marito**
my wife	**mia moglie**
my ex-husband	**il mio ex-marito**
my ex-wife	**la mia ex-moglie**
my father-in law	**mio suocero**
my mother-in-law	**mia suocera**
my brother-in-law	**mio cognato**
my sister-in-law	**mia cognata**
my partner	**il mio / la mia partner**
my friend	**il mio amico / la mia amica**
my boyfriend	**il mio ragazzo**
my girlfriend	**la mia ragazza**
my godson	**il mio figlioccio**
my goddaughter	**la mia figlioccia**
a married couple	**una coppia di sposi**
widow	**la vedova**
widower	**il vedovo**

Pet names **Vezzeggiativi**

darling	**caro/a**
darling / sweetheart	**tesoro / amore**
daddy	**papà / babbo**
mummy	**mamma**
grandpa	**nonno**
grandma, nan	**nonna**
kiddy	**bambino**

Useful verbs

to like someone	**avere simpatia per qualcuno / piacere***
to flirt	**flirtare**

to kiss	**baciare**
to go out with someone	**uscire con qualcuno**
to get on with someone	**andare d'accordo con qualcuno**
to have a good time	**divertirsi**
to have intercourse / sex	**avere rapporti sessuali**
to get married	**sposarsi**
to get on each other's nerves	**darsi ai nervi**
to look after someone	**occuparsi di**
to quarrel	**litigare**
to separate	**separarsi**
to divorce	**divorziare**

*See 1.6, 'I think, I feel'.

Useful phrases

May I introduce my ...	**Ti presento mio/mia ... / Questo/a è mio/mia ....**
Pleased to meet you	**Piacere! / Molto lieto!**
I am sorry to hear about your separation / divorce / bereavement	**Mi dispiace (sapere) che si è separato / che ha divorziato / che è in lutto.**
Will you go out with me?	**Vuoi / vuole uscire con me?**
I am going out with ...	**Esco con ...**
We are just good friends.	**Siamo solo buoni amici.**

Tips for remembering words

- Remember that lots of words for family members can be grouped in pairs – **figlio/a, cugino/a** and so on. Try to associate the words with members of your own family – you could draw your own family tree and label it.
- Think of **padre** as being a word we use for a *priest* (*Father* ...) and as being related to our word *paternal*; similarly with **madre** and *maternal*.

2.2 Children

Core vocabulary

baby	**il bebé**
infant	**il bambino piccolo / la bambina piccola**
child	**il bambino / la bambina**
boy	**il ragazzo / il bambino**
girl	**la ragazza / la bambina**
twin	**il gemello / la gemella**
teenager	**l'adolescente / il/la teenager**
adolescent	**l'adolescente**
pregnancy	**la gravidanza**
birth	**la nascita / il parto**
newborn baby	**il neonato / la neonata**
nanny	**la bambinaia**
childminder	**la bambinaia**
babysitter	**il/la babysitter**
midwife	**l'ostetrica**
crèche	**l'asilo nido**
playschool	**l'asilo**
baby's bottle	**il biberon**
teat	**la tettarella**
dummy	**il succhiotto**
bib	**il bavaglino**

babymilk	**il latte per bambini**
high chair	**il seggiolone**
nappy	**il pannolino**
carrycot	**la culla portatile**
cot	**il lettino**
pram	**la carrozzina**
pushchair	**il passeggino**
toy	**il giocattolo**
wind	**il ruttino**
colic	**la colica**
an only child	**figlio unico / figlia unica**
an adopted child	**un bambino adottivo**
an orphan	**un orfano**
children's playground	**il parco giochi**
swing	**l'altalena**
slide	**lo scivolo**
roundabout	**la giostra**

In Italy, 'family festivals' are largely like ours: events such as christenings, birthdays, weddings and funerals are important family events, at which the wider family will gather to celebrate – or commiserate – with relatives. There are special traditions attached to these events, too many to mention here. However, two extra 'special' events are celebrated in Italy:

- Many people still celebrate their **onomastico** or *saint's day* – the day dedicated to the saint whose name they carry. Thus, a Pietro will celebrate St Peter's day on June 29th, a Michele will celebrate St Michael's day, September 29th (Michaelmas); girls called Maria may celebrate dates such as August 15 and October 12, there being many feast-days devoted to the mother of Jesus.
- Many Italians are Roman Catholics, and celebrate **la Prima Comunione** *the First Communion* of their children, usually in June. You may come across other such religious events: you could ask an Italian friend to explain them, and hopefully you might understand the answer!

Useful verbs

to be expecting a baby	**aspettare un bambino**
to breastfeed	**allattare (al seno)**
to burp	**ruttare**
to change a nappy	**cambiare un pannolino**
to cry	**piangere**
to feed	**poppare**
to give a bottle	**dare il biberon**
to rock	**far dondolare / cullare**
to teethe	**mettere i denti**
to look after	**prendersi cura di**
to childmind	**sorvegliare un bambino**
to babysit	**guardare i bambini / fare il/la babysitter**

Useful phrases

I am pregnant	**sono incinta**
I'm on the pill	**prendo la pillola**
It's a boy/girl	**è un maschio / una femmina**
sibling rivalry	**la rivalità tra fratelli**
family planning	**la pianificazione familiare**
a spoilt child	**un bambino viziato**
I need	**ho bisogno di**
a cream for a sore bottom	**una pomata per irritazione da pannolini**
sun cream for children	**una crema solare per bambini**
shampoo for children	**uno shampoo per bambini**
something for wind	**qualcosa per la flatulenza**
for children teething	**qualcosa per la dentizione**

Word-building

You will notice that often one word will have another word or
words based on it; here are some examples:

child	il bambino	→ la bambinaia	nanny
to drink	bere	→ il biberon	baby's bottle
chair	sedia	→ seggiolone	high chair
to go for a walk	passeggiare	→ il passeggino	pushchair

Insight

A little-known fact is that although Italians are famously fond of children (as you will know if you have been on holiday there with any!), the birth rate there is one of the lowest in the world – so the old stereotype of Italians all having large families no longer holds true.

2.3 Anniversaries, marriage and death

Core vocabulary

birthday	il compleanno
engagement	il fidanzamento
marriage	il matrimonio
death	la morte

the wedding	le nozze / il matrimonio
church	la chiesa
town hall	il municipio

engagement ring	l'anello di fidanzamento
wedding invitation	la partecipazione di nozze
wedding day	il giorno delle nozze
wedding dress	l'abito da sposa
wedding ceremony	la cerimonia nuziale
wedding ring	la fede / vera
wedding certificate	il certificato di matrimonio
wedding cake	la torta nuziale

bride	**la sposa**
bridegroom	**lo sposo**
bridesmaid	**la damigella d'onore**
honeymoon	**la luna di miele / il viaggio di nozze**
married life	**la vita matrimoniale / coniugale**
separation	**la separazione**
divorce	**il divorzio**
silver wedding anniversary	**le nozze d'argento**
golden wedding anniversary	**le nozze d'oro**
heterosexual	**eterosessuale**
homosexual	**omosessuale**
lesbian	**lesbica**
death	**la morte**
funeral	**il funerale**
corpse	**il cadavere**
coffin	**la bara**
cemetery	**il cimitero**
burial	**il seppellimento**
cremation	**la cremazione**
grave	**la tomba**
death duties	**la tassa di successione**
death certificate	**il certificato di morte**
will	**il testamento**

Useful verbs

to get engaged	**fidanzarsi**
to get married	**sposarsi**
to die	**morire**
to be buried	**essere seppellito**
to be in mourning	**essere in lutto**
to kill yourself	**suicidarsi**

Useful phrases

Congratulations!	**Congratulazioni!**
Happy birthday	**Buon compleanno!**
Congratulations on your engagement	**Congratulazioni per il tuo fidanzamento**
wedding	**il tuo matrimonio**
anniversary	**il tuo anniversario**
We would like to wish you every future happiness	**Vi auguriamo ogni felicità per il futuro**
We would like to send you our best wishes	**Vi inviamo i migliori auguri**
I would like to convey my condolences	**Le / Vi porgo le mie più sentite condoglianze**
I am very sorry to learn of your sad loss	**Ho appreso con immense dolore della scomparsa del suo caro**

TEST YOURSELF

Identify the odd word or phrase in each series.

1 **a** mio zio **b** mia madre **c** mio cugino **d** mia borsa **e** mia nipote
2 **a** flirtare **b** baciare **c** avere rapporti sessuali **d** sposarsi
   e dichiarare
3 **a** il cadavere **b** il seggiolone **c** il bavaglino **d** il pannolino
   e la carrozzina
4 **a** la bara **b** le nozze **c** la tomba **d** il seppellimento **e** il cimitero
5 **a** la chiesa **b** la tivù **c** la fede **d** l'abito da sposa **e** la ceremonia
   nuziale
6 **a** allattare **b** mettere i denti **c** piangere **d** leggere **e** far dondolare
7 **a** l'altalena **b** lo scivolo **c** la patente di guida **d** la giostra
   e il parco giochi
8 **a** la sposa **b** l'olfatto **c** la damigella d'onore **d** la luna di miele
   e lo sposo
9 **a** babbo **b** nonno **c** mamma **d** nonna **e** Parigi
10 **a** il fratello **b** la madre **c** la sorella **d** il passeggino **e** il nipote

Answers: **1 d** mia borsa; **2 e** dichiarare; **3 a** il cadavere;
4 b le nozze; **5 b** la tivù; **6 d** leggere; **7 c** la patente di guida;
8 b l'olfatto; **9 e** Parigi; **10 d** il passeggino

3

Work

3.1 Job titles

After **sono, sei, è** etc., you don't need **un/una** in front of jobs and professions.

Core vocabulary

accountant	**il/la contabile, il ragioniere / la ragioniera**
actor/actress	**l'attore / l'attrice**
architect	**l'architetto**
builder	**il muratore**
businessman	**l'uomo d'affari, l'imprenditore**
civil servant	**l'impiegato statale**
dentist	**il/la dentista**
doctor	**il medico, il dottore / la dottoressa**
driver	**l'autista**
electrician	**l'elettricista**
engineer	**l'ingegnere**
farmer	**l'agricoltore**
farm worker	**il/la bracciante**
fireman	**il pompiere, il vigile del fuoco**
hairdresser	**il parrucchiere / la parrucchiera**
journalist	**il/la giornalista**

lawyer	**l'avvocato / l'avvocatessa**
lecturer / professor	**il professore / la professoressa**
mechanic	**il meccanico**
musician	**il/la musicista**
nurse	**l'infermiere / l'infermiera**
plumber	**l'idraulico**
policeman	**il poliziotto, l'agente di polizia**
policewoman	**la donna poliziotto**
postman	**il postino / la postina**
receptionist	**il/la receptionist**
scientist	**lo scienziato / la scienziata**
secretary	**il segretario / la segretaria**
shop assistant	**il commesso / la commessa**
shopkeeper	**il/la negoziante**
student	**lo studente / la studentessa**
waiter/waitress	**il cameriere / la cameriera**
worker	**l'operaio / l'operaia**
unemployed	**disoccupato / senza lavoro**
retired	**pensionato / in pensione**

The staff **Il personale**

chairman	**il presidente**
chief executive	**il direttore generale**
managing director	**l'amministratore delegato**
director	**il dirigente / direttore**
company secretary	**il segretario generale**
departmental head	**il capo di dipartimento**
accountant	**il ragioniere / contabile**
manager	**il dirigente / direttore**
business consultant	**il consulente commerciale**
personal assistant	**il segretario / la segretaria particolare**
employer	**il datore di lavoro**
employee	**il/la dipendente**
sales representative	**il/la rappresentante di commercio**
computer operator	**il/la terminalista**

computer programmer	il programmatore / la programmatrice di computer
secretary	il segretario / la segretaria
caretaker	il/la custode, il bidello / la bidella
cleaner	l'addetto/a alle pulizie
businessman	l'uomo d'affari
businesswoman	l'imprenditrice
trainee	l'apprendista

Areas of work **Settori di lavoro**

agriculture	l'agricoltura
banking	il settore bancario
building trade	l'industria edilizia
catering	il catering
civil service	l'amministrazione pubblica
commerce	il commercio
finance	il settore finanziario
the hotel industry	il settore alberghiero
insurance	l'assicurazione
leisure services	i servizi ricreativi
manufacturing	le industrie manifatturiere
medicine	la medicina
the media	i mass media
the public services	i servizi pubblici
purchasing	il settore acquisti
retail	il commercio al dettaglio
service industry	il settore terziario
show business	il mondo dello spettacolo
textiles	l'industria tessile
tourism	il turismo
transport	il trasporto
wholesale	il commercio all'ingrosso

Useful verbs

| to work / earn my living | lavorare / guadagnarmi da vivere |
| to be out of work | essere disoccupato |

to buy / sell	**comprare / vendere**
to import / export	**importare / esportare**
to manage	**dirigere**
to manufacture	**fabbricare**

Useful phrases

I'd like to work as / in ...	**mi piacerebbe lavorare come / in**
I work as / in	**lavoro come / in**
I used to work as / in	**lavoravo come / in**

Word building

work	**il lavoro**
to work	**lavorare**
worker (m)	**il lavoratore**
worker (f)	**la lavoratrice**
employment	**l'occupazione / l'impiego**
unemployment	**la disoccupazione**
employed	**impiegato**
unemployed	**disoccupato**

Insight

In English there has been a tendency in recent years to make words for jobs non-gender-specific (cf. *chair*, *firefighter*, etc.), largely to avoid inelegant linguistic constructions. As Italian (like most other languages) is an inflected language with ready-made feminine forms, this problem doesn't exist.

3.2 Where do you work?

Core vocabulary

I work in a/an ...	**lavoro in ...**
bank	**una banca**
factory	**una fabbrica**
farm	**una fattoria**
garage	**un'autofficina**
hospital	**un ospedale**
hotel	**un albergo**
mine	**una miniera**
office	**un ufficio**
post office	**un ufficio postale**
railways	**ferrovia**
restaurant	**un ristorante**
school	**una scuola**
service station	**una stazione di servizio**
shopping centre	**un centro commerciale**
studio	**uno studio**
town hall	**un municipio**
workshop	**un'officina**

the company	**la compagnia / società**
headquarters	**la sede centrale**
subsidiary	**la filiale**
firm	**l'azienda / ditta**
factory	**la fabbrica**
limited company	**la società a responsabilità limitata**

I work in a shop	**lavoro in un negozio**
... on a building site	**... in cantiere di costruzione**
... in a sports centre	**... in un centro sportivo**
... outdoors	**... fuori / all'aria aperta**
... indoors	**... al coperto**

3.3 The office

Core vocabulary

the premises	**il locale**
boardroom	**la sala del consiglio**
canteen	**la mensa**
meeting room	**la sala delle riunioni**
reception	**la reception**
entrance	**l'ingresso / l'entrata**
exit	**l'uscita**
security code	**il codice di sicurezza**
pass	**il lasciapassare / permesso**
I work in the ... department	**lavoro nella sezione /**
	nel reparto ...
accounts	**contabilità**
advertising	**pubblicità**
administration	**amministrazione**
after-sales	**servizio assistenza clienti**
catering	**catering**
distribution	**distribuzione**
export	**esportazione**
import	**importazione**
facilities management	**gestione di servizi**
information technology	**informatica**
insurance	**assicurazione**
manufacturing	**fabbricazione**
marketing	**marketing**
personnel / human resources	**personale / risorse umane**
property	**proprietà**
purchasing	**acquisti**
sales	**vendite**
legal department	**il reparto legale**
technical department	**il reparto tecnico**

Useful verbs

to buy	**comprare**	**compro**
to manage	**dirigere**	**dirigo**
to manufacture	**fabbricare**	**fabbrico**
to research	**fare ricerca**	**faccio ricerca**
to sell	**vendere**	**vendo**
to study	**studiare**	**studio**
to travel	**viaggiare**	**viaggio**
to work	**lavorare**	**lavoro**

Useful phrases

Where do you work?	**Dove lavori tu / lavora Lei?**
Which department do you work in?	**In quale reparto lavori / lavora Lei?**
Our head office is based in ...	**La nostra sede centrale è basata a ...**
Please sit down!	**Siediti / Si sieda per favore!**
Can I get you a coffee?	**Posso portarti / portar Le un caffè?**
Would you like to meet ...?	**Ti / Le piacerebbe fare la conoscenza di ...?**

Take care with the few words which are not quite what they appear to be:

il centralino	*switchboard*
l'interno	*extension*
l'officina	*garage* (for repairs and service)

3.4 Conditions of employment

Core vocabulary

working conditions	**le condizioni di lavoro**
the working day	**la giornata lavorativa**
the working week	**la settimana lavorativa**
holidays	**le vacanze**
annual holiday	**le vacanze annuali**
national holidays	**le feste nazionali**
pay / salary	**il salario / lo stipendio**
income	**il reddito**
income tax	**l'imposta sul reddito**
VAT	**l'imposta sul valore aggiunto / IVA**
applicant	**il candidato / la candidata**
application	**la domanda**
application form	**il modulo di domanda**
CV	**il curriculum vitae**
contract	**il contratto**
job interview	**il colloquio di lavoro**
full-time job	**il lavoro a tempo pieno**
part-time job	**il lavoro part-time**
office hours	**l'orario d'ufficio**
overtime	**il lavoro straordinario**
flexitime	**l'orario flessibile**
coffee break	**la pausa per il caffè**
lunch-time	**l'ora di pranzo**
meeting	**la riunione**
leave	**il congedo**
sick leave	**il congedo per malattia**
sick note	**il certificato di malattia**
compassionate leave	**il congedo per motivi di famiglia**
dismissal	**il congedo / licenziamento**
redundancy	**il licenziamento**

union	**il sindacato**
union meeting	**la riunione sindacale**
strike	**lo sciopero**
demand	**la rivendicazione**
bankruptcy	**il fallimento / la bancarotta**
lay-off	**il licenziamento**
standard of living	**il tenore di vita**
unemployment rate	**il tasso di disoccupazione**
legal minimum wage	**il salario minimo legale**

Useful verbs

to be behind with one's work	**essere indietro con il lavoro**
to catch up with work	**mettersi in pari col lavoro**
to be ahead	**essere in anticipo**
to have a deadline	**avere una scadenza da rispettare**
to be overworked	**lavorare troppo**
to be stressed	**essere stressato**

Useful phrases

It is stressful / stimulating	**È stressante / stimolante**
He is very efficient	**Lui è molto efficiente**
organized / disorganized	**... organizzato / disorganizzato**
hard working / lazy	**... un gran lavoratore / un pigrone**

Word building

There is often a part of the word which can give you a clue to its
meaning or help you to remember it.

il direttore	*manager*
il dirigente	*executive*
dirigere	*to manage*
la direzione	*management*

3.5 Writing a letter

- Always write your name/address on the back of the envelope, after the word **mittente** *sender*.
- Only write your town/city and the date at the top right of your letter.

Starting an informal letter

Dear Dad / brother / son / grandad	*Caro papà / fratello / figlio / nonno*
Dear Uncle David	*Caro zio Davide*
Dear Mum / sister / daughter / grandma	*Cara mamma / sorella / figlia / nonna*
Dear Aunt Anna	*Cara zia Anna*
Dear Giuseppe / Michele / Sergio	*Caro Giuseppe / Michele / Sergio*
Dear friend	*Caro amico / Cara amica*

Ending an informal letter

Love	**Cari saluti**
Write soon	**Scrivi presto**
Give my regards to your father / parents	**Salutami tuo padre / i tuoi genitori**
Give a kiss to your little brother	**Da' un bacio al tuo fratellino**
A kiss / hug (= love from ...)	**Un bacio / abbraccio (da ...)**

Starting a formal letter

Dear Mr Paolo / Mr Borletti	**Caro signor Paolo / signor Borletti**
Dear Mrs Luisa / Miss Morini	**Cara signora Luisa / signorina Morini**
Dear Sir / Madam	**Gentile Signore / Signora**
Dear ... (very formal)	**Egregio/a ...**

Ending a formal letter

Best wishes	**Cordiali saluti**
Yours sincerely (very formal)	**Distinti saluti**

3.6 Using the telephone

Core vocabulary

telephone	**il telefono**
receiver	**il ricevitore**
extension	**l'interno**
mobile	**il telefonino**
telephone number	**il numero di telefono**
directory	**l'elenco (telefonico)**
local call	**la telefonata urbana**
long distance call	**la telefonata interurbana**
international call	**la telefonata internazionale**
to phone	**telefonare**
to call	**chiamare**
to call back	**richiamare**
to divert a call	**trasferire una chiamata**
to put someone through	**mettere qualcuno in comunicazione con**
to look up a number	**cercare un numero**

Useful phrases

Hello!	**Pronto!**
Could I speak to ...?	**Vorrei parlare con/a ...**
Can I have extension ... please?	**Mi dia interno numero ... per favore.**
Can I have someone who deals with ...?	**Vorrei parlare con chi si occupa di ...**

Who is calling?	**Chi parla?**
Can you tell me what it is about?	**Mi può dire di che si tratta?**
Who would you like to speak to?	**Con chi vuole parlare?**
Speaking!	**Sono io!**
Can you wait a moment?	**Può aspettare un attimo?**
I am putting you through	**Le passo ... / La metto in comunicazione**
The line is engaged / busy	**La linea è occupata**
The line is free	**La linea è libera**
Do you want to hold?	**Vuole attendere in linea?**
Would you like to leave a message?	**Vuole lasciare un messaggio?**
Can I take your name and number?	**Mi dia il suo nome e il suo numero**
I haven't got a signal	**Non c'è ricezione**
My battery is running low	**La mia batteria si sta scaricando / è esaurita**
Can you ring back?	**Mi può richiamare?**
Can you text me?	**Mi può spedire un messaggio SMS**
Hello – this is .... call me when you can	**Pronto – sono ... Mi richiami quando può**
This is ... I'm calling to say I can't go today	**Sono ... Chiamo per dire che oggi non posso andare**
Tell your brother not to come, as there won't be a match	**Dica a suo fratello di non venire, che non ci sarà una partita**
I'm afraid we can't reserve the room you want	**Mi scusi, ma non possiamo riservare la camera che lei desidera**

3.7 Using the computer

Core vocabulary

computer	il computer
keyboard	la tastiera
mouse	il mouse
microphone	il microfono
speakers	gli altoparlanti
hard drive	l'hard disc / il disco rigido
screen	lo schermo
laptop	il laptop
printer	la stampante
scanner	lo scanner / il lettore
e-mail	la posta elettronica
world-wide web	il Web
net	la rete
code	il codice
password	la parola d'ordine
programme	il programma
modem	il modem
connector	il connettore
battery	la pila / batteria
phone jack	il jack del telefono

On the screen **Sullo schermo**

file	file / archivio
edit	editare
view	vedere / visualizzare
insert	inserire / digitare
format	formato
to format	formattare
font	il carattere
tools	utensili
table	tabella
window	finestra
work	lavoro
help	aiuto

Useful verbs

switch on	**accendere**
type in	**inserire / digitare**
log on	**aprire una sessione**
log off	**terminare una sessione**
save	**salvare**
go on line	**entrare in linea / on line**
send an e-mail	**spedire un'e-mail / un messaggio elettronico**
receive mail	**ricevere un'e-mail / un messaggio elettronico**
download a file	**trasferire un archivio / file**
recharge the battery	**ricaricare la pila / batteria**

Useful phrases

Have you got a ...	**Ha un(a) ...?**
My computer isn't working...	**Il mio computer non funziona**
Is there any one who can help me?	**C'è qualcuno che mi possa aiutare?**

Insight

Most computer language comes from American English, and Italian, like a lot of other languages, uses a lot of it. However, there are quite a few Italian words that you will need to master as well, if you want to use a computer in Italy. **La tastiera, lo schermo, la rete**, etc., are words that not only are not from English, but would also be hard to guess!

TEST YOURSELF

Match the following Italian words in the left-hand column to the English words in the right-hand one.

1	l'autista	**a**	tools
2	il cameriere	**b**	keyboard
3	il commercio all'ingrosso	**c**	bankruptcy
4	la filiale	**d**	to log on
5	il licenziamento	**e**	to call
6	la bancarotta	**f**	the wholesale trade
7	chiamare	**g**	driver
8	la tastiera	**h**	dismissal
9	utensili	**i**	waiter
10	aprire una sessione	**j**	subsidiary

Answers: 1g, 2i, 3f, 4j, 5h, 6c, 7e, 8b, 9a, 10d

4

....

Education

.....

4.1 Primary and secondary education

School attendance is compulsory in Italy from the age of 6 to 16.

Core vocabulary

headteacher (primary school)	**il direttore / la direttrice**
headteacher (secondary school)	**il/la preside**
deputy head (primary school)	**il vice-direttore / la vice-direttrice**
deputy head (secondary school)	**il/la vice-preside**
primary teacher	**l'insegnante, il maestro / la maestra**
secondary teacher	**il professore / la professoressa**
pupil	**l'allievo/a**
school secretary	**il segretario / la segretaria**
school nurse	**l'infermiere / l'infermiera di scuola**
school caretaker / janitor	**il bidello / la bidella**
lesson	**la lezione**
break	**l'intervallo**
lunch time	**l'ora di pranzo**
the bell	**il campanello**
the end of lessons	**la fine delle lezioni**
term	**il trimestre**
half term	**le vacanze di metà trimestre**

holidays	**le vacanze**
the timetable	**l'orario**

School subjects **Le materie**

Art	**il disegno**
Biology	**la biologia**
Chemistry	**la chimica**
Civics	**l'educazione civica**
English	**l'inglese**
French	**il francese**
History	**la storia**
Geography	**la geografia**
German	**il tedesco**
Information technology	**l'informatica**
Italian	**l'italiano**
Maths	**la matematica**
Music	**la musica**
P.E.	**l'educazione fisica**
Physics	**la fisica**
Science	**le scienze**
Spanish	**lo spagnolo**
Technology	**la tecnologia**

The building **L'edificio**

classroom	**la classe / l'aula**
corridor	**il corridoio**
science lab	**il laboratorio di scienze**
gym	**la palestra**
games room	**la sala giochi**
sports hall	**la palestra per gli sport di squadra**
sports centre	**il centro sportivo**
music room	**l'aula di musica**
library	**la biblioteca**
computer room	**l'aula d'informatica**
cloakroom	**il guardaroba**
changing rooms	**lo spogliatoio**
toilets	**i gabinetti**

In the classroom **Nell'aula**

desk	**la cattedra / il banco**
blackboard	**la lavagna**
projector	**il proiettore**
computer	**il computer**
white board	**la lavagna bianca**
interactive white-board	**la lavagna bianca interattiva**
overhead projector	**la lavagna luminosa**
book	**il libro**
exercise book	**il quaderno**
pencil case	**l'astuccio per matite**
pen	**la penna**
biro/ballpoint	**la biro / la penna a sfera**
pencil	**la matita**
eraser	**la gomma da cancellare**
board-rubber	**il cancellino**
calculator	**la calcolatrice**
protractor	**il goniometro**
ruler	**la riga / il righello**
report	**la pagella**
school bag	**la cartella**
sports kit	**la tenuta da sport**

Useful verbs

to read	**leggere**
to speak / talk	**parlare**
to listen	**ascoltare**
to discuss	**discutere**
to write	**scrivere**
to copy	**copiare**
to take notes	**prendere appunti**
to be quiet	**stare zitto**

Useful phrases

to do your homework	**fare i compiti**

to get a good mark	**avere un buon voto**
to sit an exam	**dare un esame**
to pass a test	**passare un esame/compito in classe**
to fail a test	**essere bocciato in un esame/compito**
to re-sit	**ripresentarsi a**
school hours	**l'orario scolastico**
progress test	**la prova di progresso**
final examination	**l'esame finale**
continuous assessment	**la valutazione continua**

Italian school students who fail their end of year exams have to spend much of the summer doing revision lessons to prepare *to re-take exams in September* essere rimandato a settembre; if they fail these exams, they have to *repeat the whole year* ripetere l'anno scolastico, and may even do so two or three times over.

4.2 Further and higher education

Core vocabulary

college	**l'istituto superiore**
technical college	**l'istituto tecnico**
university	**l'università**
faculty	**la facoltà**
class	**la classe**
lecture	**la lezione / conferenza**
seminar / tutorial	**il seminario**
professor	**il docente**
full professor	**professore ordinario**
senior lecturer	**professore associato**
student	**lo studente**
research student	**lo studente che fa della ricerca**
graduate	**il laureato**

undergraduate	**lo studente universitario**
apprentice	**l'apprendista**
trainee	**il tirocinante**
examination	**l'esame**
curriculum	**il programma**
level	**il livello**
mark / grade	**il voto**
research	**la ricerca**
candidate	**il candidato**
open / competitive examination	**il concorso**
a paper (research paper)	**la relazione**
a report	**il rapporto**
a dissertation	**la dissertazione**
a thesis	**la tesi**

Note the false friends:

a research paper (as well as a relationship)	**una relazione**
mark / grade (as well as a vote)	**un voto**
secondary teacher (as well as a university professor)	**il professore**

Useful verbs

to correct	**correggere**
to discuss	**discutere**
to explain	**spiegare**
to learn	**imparare**
to qualify	**abilitarsi**
to register/enrol	**iscriversi**
to study	**studiare**
to teach	**insegnare**
to translate	**tradurre**
to understand	**capire**

| to do research | **fare ricerche** |
| to graduate | **laurearsi** |

Useful phrases

to present a paper	**leggere una relazione**
to do a sandwich course	**fare un corso che alterna lo studio al lavoro**
to study part-time	**studiare part time**
to attend evening class	**seguire un corso serale**
to do work experience	**fare pratica nel mondo del lavoro**

Insight

Don't forget that the word **professore** in Italian is used much more widely than *professor* in English, and includes secondary school teachers as well as university staff. So if you are a teacher, don't be surprised if you are addressed as **Professore** (or **Professoressa**).

TEST YOURSELF

See how quickly you can unjumble these words from Unit 4.

1 al teamitmaca
2 li treestrim
3 li faceners
4 al lobbicatie
5 li tropetorie
6 li noderuaq
7 trasecola
8 fear i pomitic
9 l'àstirevinu
10 li toov

Answers: 1 la matematica; 2 il trimestre; 3 il francese; 4 la biblioteca; 5 il proiettore; 6 il quaderno; 7 ascoltare; 8 fare i compiti; 9 l'università; 10 il voto

Now you have unjumbled them, try to write down the English for each word in a set time (say, five minutes).

5

At home

5.1 The house

Core vocabulary

house / home	la casa
apartment / flat	l'appartamento
studio	il monolocale
block of flats	il palazzo
building	l'edificio
floor / storey	il piano
ground floor	il pianterreno
first floor	il primo piano
second floor	il secondo piano
basement	il seminterrato
attic	la mansarda
stairs	la scala
lift	l'ascensore
garage	il garage
cellar	la cantina
cottage	la villetta / il cottage
farm	la fattoria
chalet / villa	la villa
council flat	la casa popolare
semi-detached house	la casa bifamiliare
terraced house	la casetta a schiera

central heating	**il riscaldamento**
double glazing	**il doppiovetro**
gas	**il gas**
electricity	**l'elettricità**
oil	**la nafta**
water	**l'acqua**
services	**i servizi pubblici**
telephone	**il telefono**
mains sewerage	**la rete fognaria**
septic tank	**la fossa settica**
sound proofing	**l'insonorizzazione**
insulation	**l'isolamento termico**
shutters	**le imposte**
Venetian blinds	**le veneziane**
burglar alarm	**l'antifurto**
outside	**fuori**
balcony	**il balcone**
roof	**il tetto**
slates	**le tegole**
terrace	**la terrazza**
conservatory	**la serra**
garden	**il giardino**
gate	**il cancello / il portone**
path	**il sentiero**
lawn	**il prato all'inglese**
flower bed	**l'aiuola**
vegetable garden	**l'orto**
greenhouse	**la serra**
swimming pool	**la piscina**
barbecue	**il barbecue**
tennis court	**il campo da tennis**
the situation	**la situazione / l'ubicazione**
aspect	**l'aspetto / l'esposizione**
view	**la vista / la veduta**
stone	**la pietra**
brick	**il mattone**

timber	**il legname**
concrete	**il calcestruzzo**

Useful verbs

to buy	**comprare**
to sell	**vendere**
to view (a house)	**vedere**
to make an appointment	**prendere un appuntamento**
to lock up	**chiudere a chiave**

Useful phrases

it overlooks the bay	**dà sulla baia**
a central position	**una posizione centrale**
close to all services	**vicino ai servizi**
in the town centre	**nel centro città**
in the suburbs	**in periferia**
in the country	**in campagna**

5.2 Rooms

Core vocabulary

rooms	**le camere**
entrance / hall	**l'ingresso**
kitchen	**la cucina**
dining room	**la sala da pranzo**
sitting room	**il salotto / soggiorno**
bedroom	**la camera da letto**
play room	**la stanza dei giochi**
bath room	**la stanza da bagno**
cloak room (downstairs toilet)	**la toilette**
study / office	**lo studio**
landing	**il pianerottolo**
stairs	**la scala**
junk room	**il ripostiglio**

window	**la finestra**
radiator	**il radiatore**
floor	**il pavimento**
ceiling	**il tetto**
door	**la porta**
wall	**il muro / la parete**
window sill	**il davanzale**
central heating	**il riscaldamento**
water heater	**lo scaldacqua / lo scaldabagno**
lock	**la serratura**
key	**la chiave**
plug	**la spina**
socket	**la presa di corrente**
switch	**l'interruttore**
handle	**la maniglia**
fuse box	**la cassetta dei fusibili**
fuse	**il fusibile**
fuse wire	**il filo fusibile**
torch	**la torcia elettrica**
curtains	**le tende**
blinds	**le veneziane**
shutters	**le imposte**
carpet / rug	**il tappeto**
fitted carpet	**la moquette**
floor/wall tiles	**le mattonelle / piastrelle**
flooring	**il materiale per pavimentazioni**
wallpaper	**la tappezzeria**
paint	**la vernice**
paintbrush	**il pennello**
ladder	**la scala a pioli**
step ladder	**la scala a libretto**

Useful phrases

upstairs	**al piano di sopra**
downstairs	**al pianterreno**

on the first floor	**al primo piano**
in the basement	**nel seminterrato**
in the attic	**nella mansarda**
Where is the ...?	**Dov'è il/la ...?**
How does it work?	**Come funziona?**

Useful verbs

to turn / switch on	**accendere**
to turn / switch off	**spegnere**

5.3 Furniture

Core vocabulary

furniture	**i mobili**
in the sitting room	**nel salotto / soggiorno**
armchair / easy chair	**la poltrona**
settee / sofa	**il divano**
coffee table	**il tavolino**
bookcase	**la libreria / lo scaffale**
lamp	**la lampada**
pictures	**i quadri**

in the bedroom	**nella camera da letto**
bed	**il letto**
bedside table	**il comodino**
chair	**la sedia**
wardrobe	**l'armadio**
chest of drawers	**il comò / cassettone**
mirror	**lo specchio**
built-in cupboard	**l'armadio a muro**
shelves	**le mensole**

in the bathroom	**nella stanza da bagno**
bath	**il bagno**
razor	**il rasoio**
shower	**la doccia**

wash basin	il lavabo / lavandino
toilet	il gabinetto / bagno
toilet (bowl)	il vaso del gabinetto
toothbrush	lo spazzolino da denti
toothpaste	il dentifricio

5.4 Household goods

Core vocabulary

television	la televisione
television set	il televisore
video recorder	il videoregistratore
DVD player	il lettore di DVD
remote control	il telecomando

bedding	le coperte e lenzuola
pillow / pillow case	il cuscino / la federa
quilt	il piumino
quilt cover	la federa del piumino
sheet	il lenzuolo
fitted sheet	il lenzuolo con gli angoli

taps	i rubinetti
plug	il tappo
shampoo	lo shampoo
conditioner	il balsamo
hair dryer	l'asciugacapelli
soap	il sapone
towel	l'asciugamano
deodorant	il deodorante

vacuum cleaner	l'aspirapolvere (m)
duster	lo straccio per la polvere
brush	la spazzola
dustpan	la paletta
cleaning materials	i materiali per la pulizia
scrubbing brush	lo spazzolone

floor mop	**il mocio**
detergent	**il detersivo / detergente**

Useful phrases

Where is the ...?	**Dov'è il/la ...?**
It's on the table	**È sul tavolo**
under the bed	**sotto il letto**
in the armchair	**nella poltrona**
in the cupboard / drawer	**nell'armadio / nel cassetto**
Can I have a clean ...?	**Mi può dare un/a ... pulito/a?**
How does the (television) work?	**Come funziona questo televisore?**

Useful verbs

to do housework	**fare i lavori di casa**
to wash	**lavare**
to clean	**pulire**
to vacuum	**pulire con l'aspirapolvere**
to make the bed	**fare il letto**

5.5 In the kitchen

Core vocabulary

table	**il tavolo**
chair	**la sedia**
stool	**lo sgabello**
drawer	**il cassetto**
cupboard	**l'armadio**
shelf	**la mensola**
sink	**il lavello / l'acquaio**
fridge	**il frigo(rifero)**
dishwasher	**la lavastoviglie**
washing machine	**la lavatrice**

drier	**l'asciugabiancheria**
mixer / liquidizer	**il frullatore**
plate	**il piatto**
dinner plate	**il piatto piano**
bowl	**la scodella / coppetta**
salad bowl	**l'insalatiera**
dish	**il piatto**
cup	**la tazza**
saucer	**il piattino**
mug	**il tazzone**
jug	**la caraffa**
teapot	**la teiera**
sugar bowl	**la zuccheriera**
knife	**il coltello**
fork	**la forchetta**
spoon	**il cucchiaio**
teaspoon	**il cucchiaino**
soup spoon	**il cucchiaio da minestra**
dessert spoon	**il cucchiaio da dessert**
carving knife	**il trinciante**
bread knife	**il coltello per il pane**
vegetable knife	**il coltello per pelare le verdure**
sharp	**affilato**
glass	**il bicchiere**
wineglass	**il bicchiere da vino**
champagne glass	**il bicchiere da champagne**
water glass	**il bicchiere per l'acqua**
tumbler	**il bicchiere**
salt	**il sale**
pepper	**il pepe**
mustard	**la senape / la mostarda**

Insight

Don't mix up the words for a glass of wine and a wineglass (or glass of water, water glass, etc.). *A glass of wine* is **un bicchiere di vino**; *a wineglass* (= *glass for wine*) is **un bicchiere da vino.** If you ask for the second when you want the first you will end up staying thirsty!

Useful phrases

I like / dislike cooking	**mi piace / non mi piace cucinare**
I'll do the washing up	**io laverò i piatti**

Useful verbs

- In recipes, instructions are usually given in the infinitive form of the verb as in the following list.
- If a friend gives you instructions they will use the normal **tu** form ending in -i for -ere (**batti**) and -ire (**arrostisci**) verbs and a special form ending in -a for -are verbs (**mescola**).
- See also 6.7, 'Using a recipe'.

mix	**mescolare**
beat	**battere**
roast	**arrostire**
toast	**tostare**
bake	**cuocere (al forno)**
steam	**cuocere a vapore**
grill	**cuocere ai ferri / alla griglia**
barbecue	**cuocere alla brace**
peel	**pelare / sbucciare**
cut	**tagliare**
slice	**tagliare a fette**
chop	**tagliare a pezzetti**
fry	**friggere**
slightly fry	**soffriggere**

Rubbish **La spazzatura**

leftovers	**gli avanzi**
packaging	**la confezione / l'imballaggio**
plastic bags	**i sacchetti di plastica**
kitchen bin / waste bin	**la pattumiera**
bin liner / black bag	**il sacco di plastica per la spazzatura**
dustbin	**il bidone della spazzatura**
recycling	**il riciclaggio**

| bottle bank | il contenitore per la raccolta del vetro |
| compost | il concime |

5.6 Outside

Core vocabulary

garage	il garage
shed	il capanno
footpath	il sentiero
gate	il cancello / il portone
security code	il codice di sicurezza

in the garden	in giardino
flower bed	l'aiuola
lawn	il prato all'inglese
flower	il fiore
plant	la pianta
bush / shrub	il cespuglio / l'arbusto
tree	l'albero
grass	l'erba
weeds	le erbacce
herbs	le erbe aromatiche
bulbs	i bulbi

Trees **Gli alberi**	
beech	il faggio
chestnut	il castagno
elm	l'olmo
hazel	il nocciolo
holly	l'agrifoglio
oak	la quercia
sycamore	il sicomoro
willow	il salice
poplar	il pioppo
cypress	il cipresso

Flowers **I fiori**

carnation	**il garofano**
daffodil	**il trombone / la giunchiglia**
rose	**la rosa**
sweet pea	**il pisello odoroso**
tulip	**il tulipano**
mimosa	**la mimosa**
orange-blossom	**il fiore d'arancio**

Garden tools **Gli attrezzi da giardinaggio**

fork	**la forca**
hoe	**la zappa**
rake	**il rastrello**
spade	**la vanga**
trowel	**la paletta da giardiniere**
lawnmower	**il tagliaerba**
wheelbarrow	**la carriola**
garden tractor	**il trattore da giardino**
garden cultivator / rotavator	**il coltivatore**
hose	**il tubo per annaffiare**
sprinkler	**l'irrigatore**
watering can	**l'annaffiatoio**
weed-killer	**il diserbante / l'erbicida**
fertilizer	**il fertilizzante**

Insects and pests **Gli insetti e gli animali nocivi**

ant	**la formica**
bee	**l'ape** (f)
greenfly	**l'afide** (m)
housefly	**la mosca**
mosquito	**la zanzara**
spider	**il ragno**
wasp	**la vespa**

You must have seen the word **Vespa** used for a make of scooter. It isn't hard to guess why it is so called!

Garden furniture **I mobili da giardino**

barbecue	**il barbecue**
table	**il tavolo**
deck chair	**la sedia a sdraio**
lounger	**il lettino da spiaggia**
bench	**la panchina**
swing	**l'altalena**
slide	**lo scivolo**

Useful phrases

it needs to be weeded	**c'è bisogno di diserbarlo**
it needs to be watered	**c'è bisogno di annaffiarlo**
the grass needs to be cut	**bisogna tagliare l'erba**
they are ripe / not ripe	**sono / non sono maturi**
I like / dislike gardening	**mi piace / non mi piace il giardinaggio**
He/she has green fingers	**Lui/lei ha il pollice verde**
I am allergic to ...	**sono allergico a ...**
I have been stung!	**Sono stato punto!**

Useful verbs

to dig	**scavare**
to plant	**piantare**
to grow	**coltivare**
to weed	**diserbare**
to water	**annaffiare**
to pick	**(rac)cogliere**
to cut the grass	**tagliare l'erba**

5.7 Tools and DIY

Core vocabulary

drill	**il trapano**
(drill) bits	**le punte**

hammer	il martello
pincers	le tenaglie
pliers	le pinze
saw	la sega
chain saw	la motosega
screwdriver	il cacciavite
spanner	la chiave inglese
staple gun	la pistola sparachiodi
tape measure	il metro a nastro
nail	il chiodo
bolt	il bullone
nut	il dado
staple	il punto metallico
brush	la spazzola
paint brush	il pennello
scissors	le forbici
sandpaper	la carta vetrata
ladder	la scala a pioli
scaffold	l'impalcatura
tiles	le tegole (roof); le piastrelle (floor)
slates	le tegole d'ardesia
window pane	il vetro
window frame	il telaio della finestra
sliding window	la finestra a ghigliottina
shutters	le imposte
plumbing and electricity	le tubature e l'elettricità
pipe	la tubatura
tap	il rubinetto
wire	il filo (elettrico)
fuse	il fusibile
plug	la spina
socket	la presa di corrente

Insight

The word for 'screwdriver' is interesting. It is **cacciavite**, which literally means 'screw hunter'. German, French, Spanish, English and Italian all use different words to say how to turn a screw – German 'pulls' them, French 'turns' them, Spanish 'un-turns' them, English 'drives' them – and Italian, as we have just seen, 'hunts' them.

Useful phrases

Can you fix it?	**Puoi / può ripararlo?**
Yes I can!	**Sì, certo!**
to fix something to a wall	**attaccare / fissare qualche cosa al muro**
to fix /mend	**sistemare / riparare**
DIY	**il bricolage / fai da te**
DIY shop	**il negozio di bricolage**

Useful verbs

to screw	**avvitare**
to unscrew	**svitare**
to hammer	**martellare**
to nail	**inchiodare**
to drill	**forare / trapanare**
to fasten	**legare / fissare**
to cut	**tagliare**
to rub down (sandpaper)	**levigare (con carta vetrata)**
to paint	**verniciare**
to plane	**piallare**
to glue	**incollare**
to solder	**saldare**
to weld	**saldare**

TEST YOURSELF

Here are 25 words that fit into five different groups. Put five words under each of the correct group headings.

Group 1	Group 2	Group 3	Group 4	Group 5
The house	*Rooms*	*Furniture*	*In the kitchen*	*Rubbish*

i mobili
il bidone della spazzatura
il frullatore
il ripostoglio
l'armadio
la cantina
la lavastoviglie
la sala da pranzo
la toilette

i sacchetti di plastica
il concime
il letto
l'acquaio
l'imballaggio
la cucina
la lavatrice
la scala

il balcone
il frigorifero
il riciclaggio
l'appartamento
la camera da letto
la fattoria
la poltrona
la sedia

Answers:

Group 1: la fattoria, la cantina, la scala, l'appartamento, il balcone
Group 2: la cucina, la sala da pranzo, la toilette, il ripostoglio, la camera da letto
Group 3: i mobili, la poltrona, la sedia, l'armadio, il letto
Group 4: la lavastoviglie, il frigorifero, la lavatrice il frullatore, l'acquaio
Group 5: il riciclaggio, l'imballaggio, il concime, il bidone della spazzatura, i sacchetti di plastica

6

Food and drink

6.1 Parties and celebrations

Core vocabulary

an invitation	un invito
a reply	una risposta
an acceptance	un'accettazione
a refusal	un rifiuto
an excuse	un pretesto
a cake	un dolce / una torta
champagne	lo champagne
a toast	un brindisi
a present	un regalo
Cheers!	Salute! / Cin cin!

Useful phrases

let's have a party	diamo una festa
let's dance	balliamo
I would like to propose a toast	vorrei proporre un brindisi
I would like to thank our hosts	vorrei ringraziare i nostri ospiti
I've got a hangover	soffro i postumi della sbornia

Useful verbs

to party	**dare una festa**
to eat	**mangiare**
to drink	**bere**
to toast (the bride)	**proporre un brindisi (alla sposa)**
to enjoy oneself	**divertirsi**
to overindulge / have too much	**mangiare / bere troppo**
to get drunk	**ubriacarsi**
to feel sick	**avere nausea, sentirsi la nausea**

It is customary to take a gift to one's host or hostess when visiting a home in Italy; a popular choice is a selection of **pasticceria** *little cakes*.

6.2 Mealtimes

Mealtimes and eating habits in Italy are as follows:

- **la prima colazione** *breakfast* is light: usually coffee, fruit-juice, a pastry, biscuits or toast; children often have chocolate spread such as **Nutella** on bread or toast, but cereals and milk are becoming increasingly popular.
- Many people go out from work to a bar mid-morning for coffee and a bun.
- **il pranzo** *lunch* is the main meal of the day; any time from about 1 to 3 pm; usually 2/3 courses, beginning with e.g. a starter or fish, then main course, but vegetables/salad separate; often fruit for dessert; perhaps accompanied by wine, especially at weekends; often followed by a *snooze* **la siesta** if possible!
- **la cena** *dinner*; can be at any time from about 7 pm to midnight! usually a lighter meal than lunch, unless a special occasion.

Core vocabulary

meals	**i pasti**
mealtimes	**le ore dei pasti**
breakfast	**la prima colazione**
lunch	**la colazione**
picnic basket	**il cestino per il picnic**
dinner	**il pranzo**
supper	**la cena**
the menu	**la carta / il menù**
starter	**antipasto**
first course	**il primo piatto**
soup	**la zuppa / la minestra**
fish	**il pesce**
main course	**il piatto principale / forte**
side dish	**il contorno**
dessert	**il dolce**
cheese	**il formaggio**
coffee	**il caffè**

Drinks **Le bevande**

soft drink	**la bibita analcolica**
orange juice	**il succo d'arancia**
water	**l'acqua** (f)
mineral water	**l'acqua minerale**
fizzy	**gassosa / frizzante**
still	**naturale / non gassosa**
aperitif	**l'aperitivo** (m)
cocktail	**il cocktail**
sherry	**lo sherry**
gin and tonic	**il gin tonic**
red wine	**il vino rosso**
white wine	**il vino bianco**
champagne	**lo champagne**
brandy	**il brandy**
liqueur	**il liquore**

Starters **Antipasti**

starters / hors d'oeuvres	**antipasti**
mixed starters	**antipasti misti**

First courses **Primi piatti**

fish soup	**la zuppa di pesce**
minestrone	**il minestrone**
chicken soup	**la zuppa di pollo**
mushroom soup	**la zuppa di funghi**
pasta and beans in thick soup	**la pasta fagioli**
mushroom risotto	**il risotto ai funghi**
spaghetti with tomato sauce	**gli spaghetti al pomodoro**
tortellini – small filled envelopes of pasta	**i tortellini**
cannelloni – pasta tubes	**i cannelloni**
lasagna – layered pasta	**le lasagne**
gnocchi – small potato pasta dumplings	**i gnocchi**

Insight

There are reputed to be hundreds of words for different kinds of pasta in Italian. Whether this is true or not, pasta certainly forms an important part of the Italian diet – although contrary to the stereotype and to many people's expectations, it is not the main part of a meal but is usually served as a first course (**primo piatto**).

Fish and meat **Il pesce e la carne**

veal	**il vitello**
beef	**il manzo**
pork	**la carne di maiale**
lamb	**l'agnello** (m)

See also 6.6, Fish and meat.

Vegetables **La verdura**

beans	**i fagioli**
peas	**i pisellini**
artichoke	**il carciofo**
fennel	**il finocchio**
cabbage	**il cavolo**
potatoes	**le patate**
chips	**le patate fritte**

See also 6.5, Fruit and vegetables.

Desserts **I dolci**

cream	**la panna**
zabaglione	**lo zabaglione** (creamy dessert made of egg yolks, sugar and marsala)
tiramisu	**il tiramisù** (sponge soaked in coffee, topped with cream cheese and chocolate)
ice cream	**il gelato**
flavours of ice-cream	**gusti di gelato**
coconut	**il cocco**
pistachio	**il pistacchio**
strawberry	**la fragola**
raspberry	**il lampone**
vanilla	**la vaniglia**
lemon	**il limone**
chocolate	**il cioccolato**

Coffee and tea **Il caffè e il tè**

coffee	**il caffè**
coffee without milk	**il caffè**
strong black coffee	**il caffè ristretto**
weak black coffee	**il caffè lungo**
espresso	**l'espresso**
small espresso	**il caffè corto**
coffee with spirits	**il caffè corretto**

coffee with milk	**il caffelatte**
coffee with a dash of milk	**il caffè macchiato**
cappuccino	**il cappuccino**
	cappuccio (slang)
decaffeinated coffee	**il caffè decaffeinato**
with sugar	**con lo zucchero**
with sweetener	**con dolcificante**
without sugar	**senza zucchero**
tea	**il tè**
Indian tea	**il tè indiano**
China tea	**il tè cinese**
herbal tea	**l'infusione di erbe**
with milk	**con latte**
with lemon	**con limone**
with sugar	**con zucchero**

Useful phrases

I have a special diet	**seguo una dieta speciale**
I am allergic to	**sono allergico a**
I don't eat ...	**non mangio ...**
I can't eat ...	**non posso mangiare ...**
I am a vegan	**sono vegetaliano**
I am a vegetarian	**sono vegetariano**
I am diabetic	**sono diabetico**

Useful verbs

to like / dislike	**piacere / non piacere a**
I like ... (it pleases me)	**mi piace ...**
I like ... (they please me)	**mi piacciono ...**
to eat	**mangiare**
to drink	**bere**
to prefer	**preferire**
to love	**amare**

6.3 Breakfast

Core vocabulary

breakfast	**la prima colazione**
cereals	**i cereali**
wheat	**il grano / frumento**
oats	**l'avena**
barley	**l'orzo**
rye	**la segale**
bran	**la crusca**
cornflakes	**i cornflakes / fiocchetti**
muesli	**il müsli**
milk	**il latte**
semi-skimmed milk	**il latte parzialmente scremato**
fat free milk	**il latte scremato**
soya milk	**il latte di soia**
goat's milk	**il latte di capra**
cream	**la panna**
yoghurt	**lo yogurt**
bacon	**la pancetta**
eggs	**le uova***
scrambled eggs	**uova strapazzate**
poached eggs	**uova in camicia**
boiled eggs	**uova alla coque**
hard boiled eggs	**uova sode**
fried eggs	**uova fritte**

***L'uovo** is masculine in the singular, feminine in the plural, **le uova.**

sausages	**le salsicce**
tomato	**il pomodoro**
mushrooms	**i funghi**
fried	**fritti**
grilled	**alla griglia**
tinned	**in scatola**
baked beans	**i fagioli all'uccelletto**

pancake	**la frittella**
maple syrup	**lo sciroppo d'acero**
ham	**il prosciutto**
salami	**i salumi**
cheese	**il formaggio**
bread	**il pane**
white	**bianco**
brown	**integrale / nero**
granary	**con chicchi di grano interi**
wholemeal	**integrale**
sliced	**a cassetta / a fette**
organic	**biologico**
rolls	**i panini**
croissant	**il croissant / cornetto**
Danish pastries	**la pasticceria**
butter	**il burro**
margarine	**la margarina**
low fat spread	**la margarina magra**
jam	**la marmellata / confettura**
marmalade	**la marmellata d'arance**
honey	**il miele**
peanut butter	**il burro d'arachidi**
tea	**il tè**
coffee	**il caffè**
milk	**il latte**
cold milk	**il latte freddo**
hot milk	**il latte caldo**
hot chocolate	**la cioccolata calda**
fruit juice	**il succo di frutta**
orange juice	**il succo d'arancia**
freshly squeezed orange juice	**la spremuta d'arancia**

Useful phrases

I don't eat breakfast	**non faccio la prima colazione**
I only eat ...	**mangio solo ...**

I don't drink milk	**non bevo il latte**
I have my breakfast at ...	**faccio la prima colazione alle ...**

6.4 Snacks

Core vocabulary

yoghurt	**lo yogurt**
biscuit	**il biscotto**
chocolate biscuit	**il biscotto al cioccolato**
piece of cake	**una fetta di torta**
bun	**il panino dolce**
sweets (desserts)	**i dolci**
sweets (e.g. toffees)	**le caramelle**
sandwich	**il tramezzino / sandwich / panino**
in brown bread	**di pane integrale**
in white bread	**di pane bianco**
in a roll	**in un panino**
with/without mayonnaise	**con/senza maionese**
with/without salad dressing	**con/senza condimento**
salad	**un'insalata**
green salad	**un'insalata verde**
tomato salad	**un'insalata di pomodori**
mixed salad	**un'insalata mista**
Russian salad	**un'insalata russa**
potato salad	**un'insalata di patate**
pancake	**la frittella / crêpe**
pasta	**la pasta**
spaghetti	**gli spaghetti**
lasagne	**le lasagne**
pizza	**la pizza**
fish and chips	**il pesce con patate fritte**
a (ham)burger	**l'hamburger**
a cheeseburger	**il cheeseburger**

Can I offer you a cup of coffee?	**Vuoi / Vuole un caffè?**
How do you take it?	**Come lo prendi / prende?**
With milk or without milk?	**Con latte o senza?**
Do you take sugar?	**Lo prendi / prende con zucchero?**
Have you got a sweetener?	**Hai / Ha un dolcificante?**
Would you like a biscuit?	**Ti / Le piacerebbe un biscotto?**
Yes, please	**Sì, per favore**
No, thank you	**No, grazie**
I am on a diet	**Sono a dieta**
I don't take ...	**Non prendo ...**
It's too hot / cold / spicy	**È troppo caldo / freddo / piccante**
It isn't cooked properly	**Non è cucinato bene**
It is delicious!	**È delizioso!**

6.5 Fruit and vegetables

Fruit **La frutta**

apple	**la mela**
cooking apple	**la mela da cuocere**
dessert apple	**la mela da mangiare**
apricot	**l'albicocca**
banana	**la banana**
fig	**il fico**
grapes	**l'uva**
cherries	**le ciliege**
melon	**il melone**
watermelon	**il cocomero / l'anguria**
peach	**la pesca**
pear	**la pera**
plum	**la prugna**
raspberry	**il lampone**
rhubarb	**il rabarbaro**
strawberry	**la fragola**

Citrus fruits **Gli agrumi**

grapefruit	**il pompelmo**

lemon	**il limone**
lime	**il cedro**
orange	**l'arancia**

Berries **Le bacche**

blackcurrant	**il ribes nero**
blueberry / bilberry / cranberry	**il mirtillo**
gooseberry	**l'uva spina**
redcurrant	**il ribes rosso**

Exotic fruits **I frutti esotici**

avocado	**l'avocado**
coconut	**la noce di cocco**
dates	**il dattero**
kiwi fruit	**il kiwi**
mango	**il mango**
passion fruit	**il frutto della passione**
pineapple	**l'ananas**

Nuts **Frutta secca**

almond	**la mandorla**
brazil	**la noce del Brasile**
cashew	**l'anacardio**
hazelnut	**la nocciola**
peanut	**l'arachide** (f)
pistachio	**il pistacchio**
walnut	**la noce**
raisin	**l'uvetta**
sultana	**l'uva sultanina**
candied peel	**la frutta candita**

Vegetables **La verdura**

cucumber	**il cetriolo**
lettuce	**la lattuga**
radish	**il ravanello**
spring onion	**la cipollina**
tomatoes	**i pomodori**
beans	**i fagioli**
broccoli	**i broccoli**

cabbage	**il cavolo**
carrot	**la carota**
cauliflower	**il cavolfiore**
courgette	**lo zucchino**
pepper	**il peperone**
aubergine	**la melanzana**
garlic	**l'aglio**
leek	**il porro**
lettuce	**la lattuga**
mushroom	**il fungo** (pl **funghi**)
onion	**la cipolla**
potato	**la patata**
sweetcorn	**il mais**
turnip / swede	**la rapa (svedese)**
kidney beans	**i fagioli comuni**
French / green / runner beans	**i fagiolini**
broad beans	**le fave**
lentils	**le lenticchie**
pumpkin	**la zucca**
shallots	**gli scalogni**
spinach	**gli spinaci**
watercress	**il crescione**

Insight

The Italian word for *onion* is **la cipolla,** which bears a striking
resemblance to the English word **chipolata**. However, as
a chipolata is a sausage the connection is at first obscure –
except that a chipolata is a sausage containing … onions!

6.6 Fish and meat

Salt-water fish **Il pesce di mare**
anchovy	**l'acciuga / alice** (f)
cod	**il merluzzo**
haddock	**l'eglefino**

herring	**l'aringa**
mackerel	**lo sgombro**
plaice	**la passera**
sardine	**la sardina**
skate	**la razza**
sole	**la sogliola**
tuna	**il tonno**
hake	**il nasello**
jelly fish	**la medusa**
octopus	**il polpo**
red mullet	**la triglia**
sea bass	**il branzino**
squid	**il calamaro**
whiting	**il merlango**

Shellfish **I frutti di mare**

crab	**il granchio**
langoustine / lobster	**l'aragosta**
mussels	**le cozze**
oyster	**l'ostrica**
prawn	**il gambero / gamberetto**

Fresh-water fish **Il pesce d'acqua dolce**

trout	**la trota**
salmon	**il salmone**
perch	**il pesce persico**
pike	**il luccio**
eel	**l'anguilla**

Meat **La carne**

beef	**il manzo**
lamb	**l'agnello**
pork	**il maiale**
veal	**il vitello**
ham	**il prosciutto**
liver	**il fegato**
kidneys	**i rognoni**

Poultry **Il pollame**

chicken	**il pollo**
turkey	**il tacchino**
duck	**l'anatra**
goose	**l'oca**

Game **La selvaggina**

grouse	**l'urogallo / il gallo cedrone**
hare	**la lepre**
partridge	**la pernice**
pheasant	**il fagiano**
pigeon	**il piccione**
rabbit	**il coniglio**
venison	**la carne di cervo**
wild boar	**il cinghiale**

The two most famous Italian cheeses are **parmigiano** (*parmesan*) made from sheep's milk and often sprinkled in grated form on pasta; and **gorgonzola,** a creamy blue cheese which tastes far better than you'd think. In recent times, **mozzarella** (in authentic form made from buffalo milk) has been made popular by the pizza; among other great cheeses to look out for are **ricotta** a very creamy, soft cheese, and **provolone,** a mature hard cheese, often sold in its spicy form as **provolone piccante.**

6.7 Using a recipe

Making a cake **Fare una torta**

ingredients	**gli ingredienti**
flour	**la farina**
plain flour	**la farina**
self-raising flour	**la farina con lievito**
raising agent (baking powder)	**il lievito**
cornflour / potato flour	**la fecola di patate**
sugar	**lo zucchero**
butter	**il burro**
salt	**il sale**

vanilla	**la vaniglia**
almond essence	**l'essenza di mandorla**
melted chocolate	**il cioccolato fuso**
grated lemon rind	**la scorza di limone grattugiata**
the juice of an orange	**il succo di un'arancia**
chopped walnuts, hazlenuts, almonds	**le noci, nocciole, mandorle tritate**
grated chocolate	**il cioccolato grattugiato**
scales	**la bilancia**
mixing bowl	**la terrina**
wooden spoon	**il cucchiaio di legno**
mixer	**il frullatore / mixer**
grater	**la grattugia**
sieve	**il setaccio**
baking tin	**la tortiera / lo stampo**
oven	**il forno**
oven gloves	**i guanti da forno**

Making soup **Fare la zuppa / la minestra**

prepare the vegetables	**preparare la verdura**
peel the carrots	**sbucciare / pelare le carote**
chop the leeks	**tagliare i porri**
melt the butter	**fondere il burro**
add the flour	**aggiungere la farina**
stir the mixture	**mescolare / agitare la mistura**
pour in the stock	**versare il brodo**
saucepan	**la casseruola / pentola**
casserole	**la casseruola**
frying pan	**la padella**
lid	**il coperchio**
handle	**il manico**
silver foil	**la carta di alluminio / stagnola**
cling film	**la pellicola trasparente**
greaseproof paper	**la carta oleata**
plastic bags	**i sacchetti di plastica**
plastic containers	**i recipienti di plastica**

TEST YOURSELF

List the words that are to do with food and mealtimes.

1 **a** i pasti **b** lo schermo **c** il contorno **d** il dolce **e** il ricevitore
2 **a** la storia **b** la zuppa di pesce **c** i gnocchi **d** il tedesco **e** la pasta fagioli
3 **a** lo zabaglione **b** il lampone **c** la panna **d** il connettore **e** il codice
4 **a** il martello **b** il burro **c** il fusibile **d** il prosciutto **e** il formaggio
5 **a** le ciliege **b** il fico **c** il capanno **d** la pesca **e** la mela
6 **a** il pollo **b** lo scivolo **c** il tacchino **d** il trapano **e** il fagiano
7 **a** la spina **b** il cacciavite **c** la trota **d** il luccio **e** l'anguilla
8 **a** la panchina **b** il granchio **c** le cozze **d** il gamberetto **e** la rete
9 **a** riscaldare **b** cucinare **c** ascoltare **d** stare zitto **e** friggere
10 **a** un ragazzo **b** le salsiccie **c** la frittella **d** un uomo **e** la pasticceria

Answers:

1 a, c, d
2 b, c, e
3 a, b, c
4 b, d, e
5 a, b, d, e
6 a, c, e
7 c, d, e
8 b, c, d
9 a, b, e
10 b, c, e

7

....

In town

_____

7.1 The town plan and the sights

Core vocabulary

bank	**la banca**
bus station	**la stazione degli autobus /**
	l'autostazione
car park	**il parcheggio**
cinema	**il cinema**
football ground	**il campo di calcio**
hospital	**l'ospedale** (m)
hotel	**l'albergo**
library	**la biblioteca**
market	**il mercato**
post office	**l'ufficio postale / la posta**
station	**la stazione**
swimming pool	**la piscina**
tourist office	**l'ufficio turistico**
town hall	**il municipio**
the sights	**i monumenti**
bridge	**il ponte**
castle	**il castello**
cathedral	**il duomo / la cattedrale**
church	**la chiesa**
fountain	**la fontana**

monument	**il monumento**
museum	**il museo**
old town	**la città vecchia / il centro storico**
opera house	**il teatro dell'opera / il teatro lirico**
park	**il parco**
river	**il fiume**
square	**la piazza**
statue	**la statua**
theatre	**il teatro**
region	**la regione**
district	**il quartiere**
built-up area	**il centro abitato / l'abitato**
town	**il paese / la città**
suburbs	**i sobborghi / la periferia**
town centre	**il centro (città)**
industrial zone	**la zona industriale**
council offices	**gli uffici municipali**
law courts	**i tribunali / le corti di giustizia**
museum	**il museo**
police station	**il commissariato**
opening times	**l'orario di apertura**
open	**aperto/a**
closed	**chiuso/a**
holidays	**le vacanze**
bank holiday	**il giorno di festa civile**
annual holiday	**le ferie annuali**

Useful verbs

to meet	**incontrarsi / vedersi**
to look for	**cercare**
to be situated	**essere situato/a**

Useful phrases

Let's meet at the café Roma	**Ci vediamo / incontriamo al caffè Roma**
Where is it?	**Dov'è?**
It is in the centre	**È in centro**
on the main street	**sulla strada principale**
near the post office	**vicino alla posta**
opposite the bank	**di fronte alla banca**
on the market place	**sulla piazza del mercato**
beside the river	**in riva al fiume**

If you ring up to find out when the bank is open, this is the sort of message you might hear:

La banca è aperta dalle 9 alle 2 e dalle 4 alle 6 da martedì a venerdì, e dalle 9 alle 2 il sabato. La banca è chiusa il lunedì.

If you ring up to find out what is on at the cinema, this is what you might hear:

Oggi diamo il nuovo film di Roberto Benigni, 'Pinocchio'. Ci sono spettacoli alle 6, alle 8.30 e alle 11. Abbiamo biglietti da 10 euro e da 15 euro.

Insight

As you can see above, the word for *from* with times is **dalle** (**da + le**, which is feminine plural to agree with **ore**). The word for *to* is **alle** (**a + le**, again to agree with **ore**). It is very important not to confuse them. I once missed making an important telephone call because I was told the telephone exchange was open **alle sette**, and I misheard this as **dalle sette**, and went there at ten past seven … to find it shut!

7.2 Getting around town

Core vocabulary

road (between towns)	**la strada**
road / street (in towns)	**la via**
avenue	**il corso / viale**
pavement	**il marciapiede**
gutter	**il canale di scolo**
pedestrian crossing	**il passaggio pedonale**
pedestrian zone	**la zona pedonale**
traffic lights	**il semaforo**
crossing lights	**le luci del passaggio pedonale**
'green man'	**il segnale di via libera**
subway (foot passage)	**il sottopassaggio**

How do I get into town? **Come posso andare in città?**

by car	**in macchina / con la macchina**
by bus	**in autobus / con l'autobus**
by tram	**in tram / con il tram**
by subway (metro)	**in / con la metropolitana / in / con il metrò**

Where is ...? **Dov'è ...?**

the bus stop	**la fermata d'autobus**
the subway/tube station	**la stazione del metrò**

Parking the car **Parcheggiare la macchina**

car park	**il parcheggio**
multi-storey car park	**il parcheggio a più piani**
underground car park	**il parcheggio sotterraneo**
full	**completo / pieno**
spaces	**posti**
entrance	**l'entrata**
ticket machine	**il distributore (automatico) di biglietti**
change (coinage)	**la moneta / gli spiccioli**
change (money returned)	**il resto**

credit card	la carta di credito
ticket	il biglietto
exit	l'uscita
barrier	la barriera
traffic warden	il vigile urbano
one-way system	il senso unico

Useful phrases

Use the crossing	Usare il passaggio pedonale
Don't cross	Non attraversare
There's a car coming	Arriva una macchina
Wait for the green man	Aspettare la luce verde
jay walking	attraversare la strada fuori dai passaggi consentiti
Excuse me ...	Mi scusi ...
Can you tell me ...?	Mi sa dire...? / Può dirmi...?
How do I get to the station?	Per andare alla stazione?
Where is the nearest car park?	Dov'è il parcheggio più vicino?
When is the next bus?	A che ora passa il prossimo autobus?
It is forbidden ...	È proibito...
to cross the road here	attraversare la strada qui
to drop litter	lasciar cadere rifiuti / cartacce
to park	parcheggiare

Useful verbs

to walk	andare a piedi
to cross	attraversare
to turn left / right	girare a sinistra / destra
to go straight on	andare sempre dritto / diritto
to run	correre
to drive	andare in macchina
to catch the bus	prendere l'autobus
to miss the bus	perdere l'autobus

7.3 Shops and shopping

Core vocabulary

shops	**i negozi**
bakery / at the baker's	**la panetteria / dal panettiere / dal fornaio**
butcher	**il macellaio**
cake shop	**la pasticceria**
chemist	**la farmacia**
clothes shop	**il negozio di abbigliamento**
department store	**il grande magazzino**
flower shop	**il fioraio / il negozio di fiori**
hairdresser	**il parrucchiere**
hypermarket	**l'ipermercato**
market	**il mercato**
shoe shop	**il negozio di scarpe / calzature**
shopping centre / mall	**il centro commerciale**
sports shop	**il negozio dello sport**
supermarket	**il supermercato**
sweet-shop / confectioners	**il negozio di dolciumi / la pasticceria**
health food store	**il negozio di cibo macrobiotico**
newsagent's	**l'agenzia di stampa**
optician	**l'optometrista / ottico**
dry cleaner's	**la tintoria**
travel agent	**l'agenzia di viaggi**
photographic shop	**il negozio di materiale fotografico**
card shop	**il negozio di biglietti d'auguri**
store guide	**la guida del grande magazzino**
escalator	**la scala mobile**
lift	**l'ascensore**
ground floor	**il pianterreno**
first floor	**il primo piano**
bedding	**le coperte e lenzuole**
fashion	**la moda**

sportswear	**l'abbigliamento sportivo**
casual wear	**il casual**
leather goods	**(gli articoli di) pelletteria**
television and electrical goods	**televisione ed elettrodomestici**
sales person	**il commesso / la commessa**
cash desk	**la cassa**
changing room	**il camerino**
customer, client	**il/la cliente**
price	**il prezzo**
deposit	**l'acconto**
discount	**lo sconto**
reductions / sales	**riduzioni / saldi**
reduced prices	**prezzi ridotti / grandi ribassi**
clearance / closing down sale	**svendita / (vendita di) liquidazione**
bargain (offers)	**affari / occasioni**

Useful phrases

How much does it cost?	**Quanto costa?**
How are you paying?	**Come vuole pagare?**
Are you paying cash?	**Paga in contanti?**
Do you have the right change?	**Ha gli spiccioli esatti?**
Will you wrap it as a gift?	**Lo può incartare in confezione regalo?**
out of stock	**esaurito**

Useful verbs

to buy	**comprare**
to sell	**vendere**
to look for	**cercare**
to pay	**pagare**
to prefer	**preferire**
to go shopping	**andare a fare la spesa / lo shopping**
to order	**ordinare**

| to deliver | **consegnare** |
| to window shop | **andare a vedere le vetrine** |

7.4 At the supermarket

Core vocabulary

food department	**il reparto di alimentari**
fruit and vegetables	**frutta e verdura**
dairy products	**latticini**
frozen foods	**prodotti surgelati**
cleaning materials	**prodotti per le pulizie**
electrical goods	**articoli elettrici**
household appliances	**elettrodomestici**
CDs	**i CD**
videos	**i video**
wines and spirits	**vini e liquori**
drinks	**bibite**
bottle of water	**la bottiglia d'acqua**
jar of jam	**il vasetto di marmellata**
box of paper hankies	**la scatola di fazzolettini di carta**
tin of tomatoes	**la scatola di pomodori**
packet of biscuits	**il pacchetto di biscotti**
tube of toothpaste	**il tubetto di dentifricio**
assistant	**il commesso / la commessa**
basket	**il cestino**
trolley	**il carrello**
cashier	**il cassiere / la cassiera**
check out	**la cassa**

Useful verbs

to buy	**comprare**
to sell	**vendere**
to weigh	**pesare**
to look for	**cercare**
to find	**trovare**
to deliver	**consegnare**

Useful phrases

Where is / Where are ...?	**Dov'è / Dove sono ...?**
on the aisle	**nel passaggio / nella corsia**
on the shelf	**sul ripiano**
Where is the gardening section?	**Dov'è il reparto di giardinaggio?**
on the row with the ...	**nel passaggio con il/la ...**
at the far end	**in fondo**
on the left/right hand side	**a sinistra / destra**
Is there a restaurant?	**C'è un ristorante?**
What time do you shut?	**A che ora chiudete?**
Are you open on a Sunday?	**È aperto la domenica?**

Italian supermarkets and hypermarkets are no different from ours, except that there are more giant shops with an extremely wide range of products, and such out-of town hypermarkets have lots of 'satellite shops' under the same roof.

7.5 At the post office and the bank

Core vocabulary

The post office **L'ufficio postale**

letter box	**la cassetta delle lettere**
post	**la posta**
letter	**la lettera**
packet	**il pacchetto**
parcel	**il pacchetto / il pacco**
postcard	**la cartolina (postale)**
writing paper	**la carta da lettere**
envelope	**la busta**
form	**il modulo**
stamp	**il francobollo**
postman	**il postino**

phone card	**la scheda telefonica**
printed matter	**le stampe**
recorded delivery	**la lettera raccomandata**
overnight delivery	**la consegna da un giorno all'altro**
air mail	**la posta aerea**
e-mail	**la posta elettronica**

Stamps can be bought not only at a post office, but also in stationery shops, in shops which sell postcards, at newsagents and tobacconists.

The bank La banca

money	**i soldi**
cash	**i contanti**
coins	**le monete**
notes	**le banconote**
cheque book	**il libretto degli assegni**
credit card	**la carta di credito**

In Italian banks, it is normal to have to cash a cheque or traveller's cheque at one desk and to take the docket to another actually to draw the cash; nowadays, however, this should be unnecessary, as almost every bank has a cash dispenser **sportello automatico** or **bancomat**. Just make sure you are familiar with the euro!

cash machine	**lo sportello automatico / il bancomat**
a cash transfer	**il trasferimento bancario / il bonifico**
the date	**la data**
the amount	**la quantità**
signature	**la firma**
the bank code	**il numero d'agenzia della banca**
the credit card number	**il numero della carta di credito**
the expiry date	**la data di scadenza**
balance	**il saldo**
loan	**il prestito**
mortgage	**il mutuo ipotecario**

Useful phrases

insert your card	**inserire la carta**
type in your number	**digitare il numero**
wait	**attendere**
remove your card	**togliere la carta**
take your money	**prendere i soldi**
fill in the form	**riempire il modulo**
go to the counter/ cash desk	**andare alla cassa**
Where do I have to sign?	**Dove devo firmare?**
How much does it cost to send this to ...?	**Quanto costa spedire questo a ...?**

Useful verbs

to cash	**incassare**
to deposit	**depositare**
to transfer	**trasferire**
to sign	**firmare**
to fill in	**riempire**

Insight

Note that, as in French, instructions on official notices and signs are usually given with the infinitive form of the verb rather than the imperative. So you will see **inserire, digitare, togliere, prendere**, etc., instead of the imperative forms of those verbs.

TEST YOURSELF

Match the sentence-halves together.

1	A che ora	**a**	prossimo autobus?
2	È aperto	**b**	questo a Londra?
3	Ha gli	**c**	mercato.
4	Per andare	**d**	attraversare la strada qui.
5	Dov'è il parcheggio	**e**	del giardinaggio?
6	È proibito	**f**	spiccioli esatti?
7	A che ora passa il	**g**	piu vicino?
8	Quanto costa spedire	**h**	alla stazione?
9	È sulla piazza del	**i**	la domenica?
10	Dov'è il repartito	**j**	chiudete?

Answers: 1j, 2i, 3f, 4h, 5g, 6d, 7a, 8b, 9c, 10e

8

In the country

8.1 The countryside

Core vocabulary

in the countryside	**in campagna**
field	**il campo**
meadow	**il prato**
footpath	**il sentiero**
hill	**la collina**
mountain	**la montagna**
stream	**il ruscello**
river	**il fiume**
lake	**il lago**
valley	**la valle**
grass	**l'erba**
plant	**la pianta**
wild flowers	**i fiori selvatici**
moss	**il muschio**
fungi	**i funghi / le muffe**
fern	**la felce**
bush	**il cespuglio**
tree	**l'albero**
wood	**il bosco**
forest	**la selva / foresta**

hedge	la siepe
fence	lo steccato / il recinto
ditch	il fosso
gate	il cancello
spring	la sorgente
pond	lo stagno
bridge	il ponte
waterfall	la cascata
weir	lo sbarramento
water mill	il mulino ad acqua
reservoir	il bacino idrico
dam	la diga
hydro electric power station	la centrale idroelettrica
flood	l'inondazione, lo straripamento
copse	il boschetto
beech	il faggio
chestnut tree	il castagno
elm	l'olmo
oak	la quercia
sycamore	il sicomoro
willow	il salice

Useful phrases

Where shall we go?	Dove andiamo?
What shall we do?	Cosa facciamo?

Useful verbs

to go for a walk	andare a fare quattro passi
to go for a long walk	andare a fare una lunga passeggiata
to go swimming	andare a nuotare
to swim	nuotare
to go hiking	fare un'escursione a piedi
to ride a bike	andare in bicicletta

to go fishing	**pescare / andare a pesca**
to flood	**inondare / straripare**

8.2 In the mountains

Core vocabulary

hill	**la collina**
mountain	**la montagna**
mountain range	**la catena di montagne**
mountain pass	**il passo / la gola**
mountain path	**il sentiero di montagna**
mountain railway	**la funicolare**
mountain hut / refuge	**il rifugio di montaga**
cable car	**la funivia**
summit	**la cima**
peak	**la cima / la vetta**
rock face	**la parete di roccia**
slope	**il pendio / versante**
gorge	**la gola**
cave	**la caverna**

The weather **Il tempo**

cloudy	**nuvoloso**
rainy	**piovoso**
sunny	**soleggiato / assolato**
it's sunny	**c'è il sole**
dry	**secco**
windy	**ventoso**
it's windy	**c'è vento**
easy	**facile**
of moderate difficulty	**abbastanza difficile**
difficult	**difficile**
of extreme difficulty	**di estrema difficoltà**

Equipment **L'attrezzatura**

rope	**la corda / la fune**

harness	l'imbracatura
karabiner	il moschettone
rucksack	lo zaino / il sacco da montagna
torch	la torcia elettrica / lampadina tascabile
stove	la cucina / stufa
dried food	alimenti liofilizzati / disidratati
waterproofs	gli impermeabili
pen knife	il temperino
water bottle	la borraccia
sleeping bag	il sacco a pelo
tent	la tenda

Useful verbs

to climb	salire
to abseil	discendere a corda doppia
to bivouac	bivaccare
to hike	fare un'escursione a piedi
to rock climb	fare roccia
to boulder	arrampicarsi su massi / fare sassismo
to ice climb	arrampicarsi su ghiaccio

Useful phrases

What is the forecast?	Come sono le previsioni del tempo?
How difficult is it?	Quant'è difficile?
How long does it take?	Quanto tempo ci vuole?

8.3 At the seaside

Core vocabulary

| sea-side (resort) | la stazione balneare |
| at the seaside | al mare |

sea	**il mare**
ocean	**l'oceano**
wave	**l'onda**
harbour / port	**il porto**
beach	**la spiaggia**
sand	**la sabbia**
sand dune	**la duna (di sabbia)**
cliff	**la scogliera**
shell	**la conchiglia**
pebbles	**i ciottoli**
rock	**la roccia**
little island	**l'isola piccola**
island	**l'isola**
jetty	**l'imbarcadero**
pier	**il pontile**
quay	**la banchina**
reef	**la scogliera**
surf	**i cavalloni / la spuma**
shore	**la riva**
coast	**il litorale**
estuary	**l'estuario**
cape	**il capo**
promontory	**il promontorio**
peninsula	**la penisola**

Boats **Imbarcazioni**

boat	**la barca / il battello**
rowing boat	**la barca a remi**
yacht	**lo yacht**
dinghy	**il dinghy / canotto**
motor boat	**il motoscafo**
steamer / waterbus	**il vaporetto**
ferry boat	**il traghetto**
car ferry	**la nave-traghetto**
cruiser	**l'incrociatore**
liner	**il transatlantico**

Sailing **La navigazione a vela**

navigation	la navigazione
port	babordo
starboard	tribordo
buoy	la boa / il gavitello
light house	il faro
mast	l'albero
sail	la vela
rudder	il timone
anchor	l'ancora
satellite positioning	navigazione satellitare
automatic pilot	il pilota automatico
ropes	le cime / i cavi

The sea **Il mare**

high tide	la marea alta
low tide	la marea bassa
sea-level	il livello del mare
calm	sereno / tranquillo
choppy	mosso / agitato
rough	grosso / tempestoso
sea floor	fondo marino
sandy	sabbioso
rocky	roccioso
rough	scabro
smooth	liscio

Useful verbs

to row	remare
to sail	navigare / veleggiare
to motor	navigare a motore
to tie up	ormeggiare
to anchor	ancorarsi
to cast off	levare gli ormeggi
to weigh anchor	levare l'ancora

to set sail	**salpare**

Useful phrases

When is high tide?	**Quando è l'alta marea?**
Where can I moor?	**Dove posso ormeggiare?**

8.4 Working in the countryside

Core vocabulary

agriculture	**l'agricoltura**
bee keeping	**l'apicoltura**
game keeper	**il guardacaccia**
horticulture	**l'orticoltura**
fruit growing	**la frutticoltura**
vine growing	**la viticoltura**
forestry	**la selvicoltura**
farm	**la fattoria**
market garden	**l'orto (industriale)**
farmhouse	**la cascina / fattoria**
barn	**il granaio**
stable / cattle shed	**la stalla**
stables (establishment)	**la scuderia**

Cattle **Il bestiame**

cows, heifer, bull, calf	**le mucche, la giovenca, il toro, il vitello**
sheep/ewe, ram, lamb	**la pecora, l'ariete, l'agnello**
pig, sow, boar, piglet	**il maiale/porco, la scrofa, il verro, il porcellino**
goats, nanny, billy, kid	**le capre, la capra, il capro, il capretto**
sheep/guard dog	**il cane da pastore/da guardia**
dog, bitch, puppy	**il cane, la cagna, il cagnolino**

Insight

Unlike English (which tends to use only one word for each type of animal) and French (which tends to use the same word for the animal in living and food form), Italian uses a variety of different words for household and farm animals, depending on their gender, type, role, etc. (e.g. **il cane, la cagna, il cagnolino**).

Poultry **Il pollame**

hen	**la gallina**
chicken	**il pollo**
duck, duckling	**l'anatra, l'anatroccolo**
goose, gosling	**l'oca, il papero**
turkey	**il tacchino**
pheasant	**il fagiano**

Crops **Il raccolto**

cereals	**i cereali**
grain	**il grano**
barley	**l'orzo**
oats	**l'avena**
rice	**il riso**
rye	**la segala**
wheat	**il frumento**
hay	**il fieno**
straw	**la paglia**

Farm jobs **Lavori nella fattoria**

farmshop	**il negozio di prodotti della fattoria**
bee keeper	**l'apicoltore**
farmer	**l'agricoltore / il coltivatore**
farm worker / peasant	**il contadino / il bracciante**
horticulturalist	**l'orticoltore**
vet	**il veterinario**
vine grower	**il viticoltore**
vineyard	**la vigna / il vigneto**
vine	**la vite**
grapes	**l'uva**

cultivating	**la coltivazione / la coltura**
planting	**piantare e seminare**
spreading fertilizer	**la fertilizzazione / concimazione**
weeding	**la diserbatura**
harvesting	**la mietitura / il raccolto**
packaging	**l'imballaggio**

Farm machinery **Le macchine agricole**

tractor	**il trattore**
trailer	**il rimorchio**
plough	**l'aratro**
combine harvester	**la mietitrebbia**

Farm shop signs **Cartelli nella fattoria**

fresh olive oil	**olio d'oliva fresco**
wine tasting	**degustazione di vini**
farmhouse cheese	**formaggio di propria produzione**
goat's cheese	**formaggio di capra**

Useful verbs

to feed	**nutrire, dare da mangiare a**
to milk	**mungere**
to raise / breed	**allevare / far riprodurre**
to sow	**seminare**
to fertilize	**fertilizzare / concimare**
to weed	**diserbare**
to pick	**(rac)cogliere**
to harvest	**mietere / raccogliere**
to take to market	**portare al mercato**

Useful phrases

Beware of the dog / bull!	**Attenti al cane / toro!**
Please shut the gate	**Si prega di chiudere il cancello**
electric fence	**la recinzione elettrica**
No entry	**Vietato l'ingresso**

TEST YOURSELF

How quickly can you match together these halves of words from Chapter 8?

1	l'imbar	**a**	mento
2	il promo	**b**	ino
3	la viti	**c**	azione
4	la borr	**d**	ntorio
5	lo za	**e**	ggia
6	l'inond	**f**	coltura
7	la funi	**g**	cia
8	lo sbarra	**h**	cadero
9	la quer	**i**	accia
10	la spia	**j**	colare

Answers: 1h, 2d, 3f, 4i, 5b, 6c, 7j, 8a, 9g, 10e

9

Hobbies and sports

9.1 Hobbies

Core vocabulary

What do you like doing?	**Che cosa ti piace fare?**
I like ...	**mi piace ...**
acting	**recitare**
cooking	**cucinare**
dancing	**ballare**
modern	**balli moderni**
ballroom	**il ballo liscio**
DIY	**il faidate**
drawing	**disegnare**
gardening	**fare giardinaggio**
going for a walk	**fare quattro passi**
going out (socially)	**uscire**
horse riding	**andare a cavallo**
listening to music	**ascoltare musica**
meeting people	**fare la conoscenza della gente**
painting	**dipingere / pitturare**
photography	**fotografare**
playing tennis / football*	**giocare a (tennis / calcio)**
pottery	**fare ceramica**
reading	**leggere**

sailing	**andare in barca a vela**
sewing	**cucire**
singing	**cantare**
sport	**fare sport**
walking	**camminare**
watching films	**guardare un film**
watching television	**guardare la televisione / la tivù**
writing	**scrivere**

*See also 9.2, Sports.

Outdoor pursuits **Le attività all'aria aperta**

birdwatching	**il bird-watching**
fishing	**pescare / la pesca**
hunting	**cacciare / la caccia**
shooting	**andare a caccia / tirare**
rambling / hiking	**fare escursioni a piedi**
archaeology	**l'archeologia**
astronomy	**l'astronomia**
history	**la storia**
visiting historical sites	**visitare i siti storici**
touring	**viaggiare / fare un giro**

Indoors **Al coperto**

playing chess	**giocare a scacchi**
playing cards	**giocare a carte**
playing bridge	**giocare a bridge**
playing bingo	**giocare a tombola**
doing jigsaw puzzles	**fare i puzzle**
playing dominoes	**giocare a domino**
playing draughts	**giocare a dama**
billiards / snooker	**giocare a biliardo**
playing table football	**giocare a calcetto**
doing crosswords	**fare i cruciverba**

Italian uses a word for *at* in phrases talking about playing things, as does French. So you say play *at* football (**giocare a calcio**) in Italian, and this corresponds to 'jouer au football' in French.

Making music **Fare musica**

playing in an orchestra	**suonare in un'orchestra**
singing in a group / a choir	**cantare in un gruppo / un coro**
playing an instrument	**suonare uno strumento musicale**
piano	**il piano(forte)**
guitar	**la chitarra**
violin	**il violino**
trumpet	**la tromba**
drums	**la batteria**

Useful verbs

to attend	**assistere a / partecipare a**
to be a member of	**essere socio di**
to be interested in	**interessarsi di**
to be keen on	**essere appassionato di**
to enjoy	**piacere a (mi piace)**
to enjoy oneself	**divertirsi**
to meet	**incontrare / fare la conoscenza di**
to spend my time	**passare il tempo**

Useful phrases

What do you do in your free time?	**Cosa fai / fa nel tempo libero?**
Do you like ...?	**Ti / Le piace ...?**
I like meeting people	**Mi piace trovarmi con altre persone**
I do (painting)	**Faccio (la pittura)**
I belong to a club	**Sono socio di un club**
We meet every ...	**Ci vediamo ogni ...**
It's interesting	**È interessante**

It's fantastic	È fantastico
It's boring	È noioso
I am interested in ...	Mi interessa ...

9.2 Sports

Ball games **yiochi di pallone**	
football	**il calcio**
footballer	**il calciatore**
ball	**il pallone**
team	**la squadra**
goal	**il gol**
match	**la partita**
football ground	**il campo di calcio**
stadium	**lo stadio**
score	**il punteggio / i punti**
rugby	**il rugby**
player	**il giocatore**
pitch	**il campo di rugby**
to score a try	**segnare una meta**
basketball	**la pallacanestro**
basket	**il canestro**
volleyball	**la pallavolo**
net	**la rete**
hockey	**l'hockey**
hockey stick	**il bastone da hockey**
golf	**il golf**
golf club	**la mazza da golf**
golf course	**il campo di golf**
green	**il green**
hole	**la buca**
bunker	**il bunker**

Racket games **I giochi di racchetta**	
tennis	**il tennis**
tennis racquet / racket	**la racchetta da tennis**
tennis court	**il campo da tennis**

tennis ball	**la palla da tennis**
tennis player	**il giocatore di tennis**
badminton	**il badminton**
net	**la rete**
shuttlecock	**il volano**
squash	**lo squash**
squash court	**il campo da squash**
squash racquet	**la racchetta da squash**
(Italian) bowls	**il gioco delle bocce**

Martial arts **Le arti marziali**

boxing	**il pugilato / la boxe**
judo*	**il judo**
karate*	**il karatè**
tae-kwando*	**il tae-kwando**
wrestling	**la lotta libera**

*Most of these sports keep the same name as in their country of origin.

Non-team sports **Gli sport individuali**

athletics	**l'atletica**
running	**la corsa**
cross country	**il cross country / la corsa campestre**
jumping	**il salto / saltare**
hurdles	**la corsa a ostacoli**
track	**la pista**
timekeeper	**il cronometrista**
gymnastics / keep fit	**la ginnastica**
aerobics	**l'aerobica**
jogging	**il jogging**
weight lifting	**il sollevamento pesi**
weight training	**l'allenamento con i pesi**
yoga	**lo yoga**

Useful verbs

to win	**vincere**

to lose	perdere
to draw	pareggiare
to box	fare il pugile
to do	fare
to jog	fare jogging
to run	correre

Football is, of course, the sport which arouses most passion across Italy, and the national team, **gli Azzurri** *the Blues*, consistently achieve high status in international competitions. The Italian league is among the most expensive and best in quality in the world; great teams such as Inter, Roma, Lazio, Juventus, AC Milan and Napoli are famous worldwide. Second to football in terms of national pride is **Formula 1** motor racing, with the red of Ferrari, with its prancing horse crest rivalling the blue football shirts for the top position among Italian icons. Cycling is another major national sport: cyclists compete for the **maglia rosa**, *the pink jersey*, in the **Giro d'Italia** and the **maglia gialla**, *the yellow jersey*, in the **Giro di Francia**.

9.3 More sports

Water sports **Gli sport acquatici**

canoeing	**il canottaggio**
canoe	**la canoa**
paddle	**la pagaia**
diving (deep sea)	**il tuffo / l'immersione (a grande profondità)**
wet suit	**la muta (da subacqueo)**
dry suit	**la sottomuta**
gas bottles	**le bombole del gas**
mask	**la maschera**
flippers	**le pinne**
snorkel	**il boccaglio**

rowing	**il canottaggio**
boat	**la barca**
oars	**i remi**
sailing	**la vela**
sail	**la vela**
surfing	**il surf / surfing**
surf board	**la tavola da surf**
waterskiing	**lo sci acquatico**
windsurfing	**il windsurf**
wind surfer	**il windsurfista**
yachting	**la navigazione da diporto**
yacht	**lo yacht**
dinghy	**il dinghy / canotto**
swimming	**il nuoto**
breast stroke	**il nuoto a rana**
front crawl	**lo stilo libero / il crawl**
butterfly	**il nuoto a farfalla**
backstroke	**il dorso**
diving	**il tuffo / i tuffi**
swimming pool	**la piscina**
length	**la lunghezza**
diving board	**il trampolino**
swimming costume	**il costume da bagno**
goggles	**gli occhiali**

Other sports **Altri sport**

archery	**il tiro con l'arco**
bow	**l'arco**
arrow	**la freccia**
target	**il bersaglio**
cycling	**il ciclismo**
racing bike	**la bicicletta da corsa**
mountain bike	**la mountain bike**
bike	**la bicicletta**
handlebars	**il manubrio**
saddle	**la sella / il sellino**
saddle bag	**la borsa**

fencing	**la scherma**
foil	**il fioretto**
horse riding	**l'equitazione** (f)
saddle	**la sella**
bridle	**la briglia**
stirrups	**le staffe**
rollerskating	**il pattinaggio a rotelle**
skates	**i pattini a rotelle**
skateboarding	**fare lo skateboard**
skateboard	**lo skateboard**
climbing / mountaineering	**l'alpinismo**
rock climbing	**la roccia**
potholing / caving	**l'esplorazione speleological**
climbing boots	**gli scarponi da montagna**
rope	**la corda / fune**
karabiner	**il moschettone**
rucksack	**lo zaino**

Winter sports Gli sport invernali

skiing	**lo sci**
skis	**gli sci**
poles	**i bastoni**
piste	**la pista**
snowboarding	**fare lo snowboard**
snowboard	**snowboard**
sledging	**andare in slitta**
sledge	**la slitta**
toboganning	**andare in slittino**
toboggan	**lo slittino**
ice skating	**il pattinaggio**
skates	**i pattini**
ice rink	**la pista di pattinaggio**

Useful phrases

I enjoy doing ...	**Mi piace molto fare ...**
I am good at ...	**Sono bravo in ...**
I am not good at ...	**Non sono bravo in ...**

TEST YOURSELF

Delete the repetitions of the first letter in each example to work out what the words are. Then write the English.

1 bfbabrbeb bgbibabrbdbibnbabgbgbibob
2 kpkiktktkukrkakrkek
3 mgmumamrmdmamrmem mlmam mtmimvmùm
4 dfdadrded dqdudadtdtdrdod dpdadsdsdid
5 uguiuoucuaurueu uau usucuaucucuhuiu
6 gfgagrgeg gig gcgrgugcigvgegrgbgag
7 xixlx xpxaxtxtxixnxaxgxgxixox xax xrxoxtxexlxlxex
8 jajnjdjajrjej jijnj jsjljijtjtjijnjoj
9 fcfafnftfafrfef fifnf fufnf fcfofrfof
10 oaonodoaoroeo oao ocoaococoioao

Answers:
1 fare giardinaggio – to do gardening
2 pitturare – to paint
3 guardare la tivù – to watch the TV
4 fare quattro passi – to go for a walk
5 giocare a scacchi – to play chess
6 fare i cruciverba – to do the crossword
7 il pattinaggio a rotelle – roller-skating
8 andare in slittino – to go tobogganing
9 cantare in un coro – to sing in a choir
10 andare a caccia – to go hunting

10

Clothing

10.1 Garments and styles

Ladies' fashion **La moda femminile**

blouse	**la blusa / camicetta**
cardigan	**il cardigan**
dress	**il vestito**
evening dress	**l'abito da sera**
sun dress	**il prendisole**
jacket	**la giacca**
long jacket	**la giacca lunga**
short jacket	**la giacca corta**
jersey	**la maglia**
shorts	**i calzoncini / gli shorts**
skirt	**la gonna**
suit	**l'abito**
trouser suit	**il completo pantalone**
trousers	**i pantaloni / calzoni**
lingerie	**la biancheria intima / lingerie**
bra	**il reggipetto / reggiseno**
knickers	**le mutandine**
slip	**la sottoveste**
stockings	**le calze**
tights	**il collant**
nightie	**la camicia da notte**

pyjamas	**il pigiama**
negligee	**il négligé / la vestaglia**

Men's fashion **La moda maschile**

blazer	**il blazer**
jacket	**la giacca**
dinner jacket	**lo smoking**
jeans	**i jeans**
jumper	**il maglione**
pullover	**il pullover**
shirt	**la camicia**
shorts	**i calzoncini / gli shorts**
socks	**i calzini**
suit	**l'abito**
sweatshirt	**la felpa**
T-shirt	**la maglietta**
tie	**la cravatta**
trousers	**i pantaloni / calzoni**
belt	**la cintura**
braces	**le bretelle**
waistcoat	**il panciotto**
boxer shorts	**I calzoncini**
underpants	**lo slip / le mutande**
vest	**la maglia / la canottiera**
pyjamas	**il pigiama**

Outerwear **I vestiti per uscire**

coat	**il cappotto / soprabito**
raincoat	**l'impermeabile**
jacket	**la giacca**
hat	**il cappello**
scarf	**la sciarpa**
gloves	**i guanti**

Useful verbs

to wear	**portare / indossare**
to fit	**andare bene (di misura)**
to suit	**stare bene**

Useful phrases

I will be wearing ...	**porterò / indosserò ...**
a dark suit	**un abito scuro**
a coat and hat	**un soprabito e un cappello**
a sweatshirt, jeans and	**una felpa, i jeans e delle**
trainers	**scarpe da ginnastica**
What will you be wearing?	**Che cosa porterai?**
What size are you?	**Che taglia porti / porta?**
it is too short	**è troppo corto**
it is too wide	**è troppo largo**
it is too long	**è troppo lungo**
it is too tight	**è troppo stretto**
Have you got anything	**Ha qualcosa di più**
bigger / smaller?	**grande / piccolo?**
in a different colour?	**in un colore diverso?**
it suits you / it doesn't suit you	**Le sta bene / non Le sta bene**

10.2 The garment

Measurements **Le misure**

tape measure	**il metro a nastro**
length	**la lunghezza**
width	**la larghezza**
size	**la taglia**

Parts of the garment **Parti dell'indumento**

collar	**il collo / colletto**
neck	**il collo**
shoulders	**le spalle**

sleeves	**le maniche**
chest	**il petto**
waist	**la vita**
cuffs	**i polsini**

Materials **Le stoffe**

fabric	**la stoffa**
it is made in ...	**è fatto di ...**
cotton	**il cotone**
fur	**la pelliccia**
artificial fur	**la pelliccia artificiale**
jersey	**il jersey**
leather	**il cuoio**
linen	**(la tela di) lino**
satin	**il raso / satin**
silk	**la seta**
suede	**la pelle scamosciata**
synthetic fibre	**la fibra sintetica**
tweed	**il tweed**
velvet	**il velluto**
wool	**la lana**

Patterns **Motivi**

it is	**è ...**
floral	**a fiori**
folded	**piegato**
multi-colour	**multicolore**
patterned	**a disegni**
pleated	**a pieghe**
plain (one colour)	**in tinta unica**
self-coloured	**monocromatico**
spotted	**a pallini**
striped	**a righe / strisce**

Repairs **Riparazioni**

button	**il bottone**
cotton	**il filo**
fastener	**la chiusura / il fermaglio**

needle	l'ago
thimble	il ditale
ribbon	il nastro
scissors	le forbici
sewing machine	la macchina da cucire
velcro	il velcro
zip	la cerniera (lampo) / lo zip

Washing **Lavaggio**

detergent	il detersivo / detergente
detergent for wool	il detersivo per lana
fabric softener	l'ammorbidente (m)
soap powder	il detersivo in polvere

Useful verbs

to wash	lavare
to dry	asciugare
to dry clean	lavare a secco
to iron	stirare
to mend	rammendare

Useful phrases

I have lost a button	Ho perso un bottone
Can I get this laundered / dry cleaned / pressed (ironed)?	Posso far lavare / far lavare a secco / far stirare questo?
How long will it take?	Quanto tempo ci vuole per farlo?
Can you remove this stain?	Può smacchiare questo?
Can you sew this button on?	Può attaccare questo bottone?
Can you take it in?	Lo/la può stringere?
Can you shorten it?	Lo/la può accorciare?

This garment must be dry cleaned	Pulire a secco
This garment can be machine washed	Lavabile in lavatrice
Handwash only	Lavare solo a mano
Don't use bleach	Non usare decolorante

10.3 Special occasions

Going to work **Al lavoro**

uniform	**l'uniforme** (f)
apron	**il grembiule**
overall	**il camice**

It's raining! **Piove!**

rain coat	**l'impermeabile**
rain hat	**il cappello impermeabile**
waterproof trousers	**i pantaloni impermeabili**
rubber boots	**gli stivali di gomma**
umbrella	**l'ombrello**

It's cold! **Fa freddo!**

anorak	**la giacca a vento**
walking boots	**gli scarponi da montagna**
thick socks	**i calzettoni**
woolly hat	**il cappello di lana**
gloves	**i guanti**

On the beach **Sulla spiaggia**

swimming costume	**il costume da bagno**
bikini	**il bikini**
trunks	**i calzoncini da bagno**
flippers	**le pinne**
goggles	**la maschera / gli occhiali**
snorkel	**il boccaglio**
flip flops	**gli infradito**

sun tan cream	**la crema solare**

A night on the town Una bella serata fuori

evening dress	**l'abito da sera**
high heels	**i tacchi alti**
smart clothes	**i vestiti eleganti**

Playing a game Fare una partita

baseball hat	**il cappello di baseball**
polo shirt	**la polo**
shorts	**i calzoncini**
socks	**i calzini**
trainers	**le scarpe da ginnastica**
sweatshirt	**la felpa**
T-shirt	**la maglietta**

For a party Per una festa

formal dress	**l'abito da cerimonia**
casual dress	**il (vestito) casual**

Jewellery I gioielli

bracelet	**il braccialetto**
brooch	**la spilla**
earrings	**gli orecchini**
necklace	**la collana**
ring	**l'anello**
watch	**l'orologio**

silver	**l'argento**
gold	**l'oro**
platinum	**il platino**
diamond	**il diamante**
emerald	**lo smeraldo**
ruby	**il rubino**
sapphire	**lo zaffiro**
semi-precious stone	**la pietra semipreziosa**

Useful verbs

to wear | **portare**

Useful phrases

He/she always looks | **Ha sempre un aspetto ...**
  casual | **casual**
  fashionable | **alla moda**
  smart | **elegante**
  unfashionable | **fuori moda**
  untidy | **disordinato**

10.4 Footwear

Core vocabulary

the shoe shop | **il negozio di calzature / scarpe**
hosiery | **il reparto calze e calzini**
socks | **i calzini**
stockings | **le calze**
tights | **il collant**
leggings | **i pantacollant / fuseaux**
I would like a pair of ... | **vorrei un paio di ...**
boots | **stivali**
clogs | **zoccoli**
flip flops | **infradito**
moccasins | **moccassini**
sandals | **sandali**
shoes | **scarpe**
slip-ons | **scarpe senza allacciatura**
slippers | **pantofole / ciabatte**
tennis shoes | **scarpe da tennis**
trainers | **scarpe da ginnastica**
wellingtons / rubber boots | **stivaloni di gomma**

ballet shoes | **le scarpe da balletto**

climbing boots	**gli scarponi da alpinismo**
cycling shoes	**le scarpe da ciclismo**
dancing shoes	**le scarpe da ballo**
diving boots	**le scarpe da tuffatore**
flippers	**le pinne**
ski boots	**gli scarponi da sci**
snowboard boots	**gli scarponi da snowboard**
steel tipped boots	**gli scarponi / stivali a puntali di acciaio**
walking boots	**gli scarponi da montagna**
leather	**il cuoio**
rubber	**la gomma**
synthetics	**le fibre sintetiche**
high-heeled shoes	**le scarpe a tacchi alti**
flat shoes	**le scarpe a tacchi bassi**
shoe polish	**il lucido da scarpe**
shoe cleaner	**la spazzola / lo strofinaccio per le scarpe**
shoe protector	**il liquido impermeabilizzante per scarpe**
shoe stretcher	**la forma (per scarpe)**
chiropody	**la chiropodia**
massage	**il massaggio**
reflexology	**la riflessologia**
foot	**il piede**
toe	**il dito del piede**
ankle	**la caviglia**
sole	**la pianta del piede**
toe nails	**le unghie del piede**
arch of the foot	**l'arco plantare**

Useful verbs

to try shoes on	**provare le scarpe**
to put on your shoes	**mettersi le scarpe**
to take off your shoes	**togliersi le scarpe**
to get blisters	**farsi venire le vesciche**

Useful phrases

bare foot	**a piedi scalzi / nudi**
I have got sore feet	**Mi fanno male i piedi**
I have got blisters	**Ho le vesciche**
Have you got a plaster?	**Ha un cerotto?**
Please remove your shoes in the house	**Per favore, togliti le scarpe quando sei in casa**
What shoe size are you?	**Che numero di scarpe porti / porta?**
These shoes are comfortable / uncomfortable	**Queste scarpe sono comode / scomode**

TEST YOURSELF

To decipher these words, write down the letter in the alphabet that comes AFTER each letter in them (z = a). Then write the English words.

abcdefghijklmnopqrstuvwxyz

1 kd ltszmchmd
2 kz bzlhbdssz
3 kz fhzbbz
4 kd rozkkd
5 kz rsneez
6 zrbhtfzqd
7 kz bnkkzmz
8 hk btnhn
9 kd rbzqod z szbbgh zksh
10 kz bzuhfkhz

Answers:
1 le mutandine – knickers
2 la camicetta – blouse
3 la giacca – jacket
4 le spalle – shoulders
5 la stoffa – fabric
6 asciugare – to dry
7 la collana – necklace
8 il cuoio – leather
9 le scarpe a tacchi alti – high-heeled shoes
10 la caviglia – ankle

11

Travel

11.1 Travel

Core vocabulary

journey	**il viaggio**
itinerary	**l'itinerario**
route	**l'itinerario / il percorso**
map	**la mappa / cartina**
overland	**per (via di) terra**
by air / plane	**in aereo**
by sea	**per mare**
by rail / train	**in treno**
by coach	**in pullman**
by car	**in macchina**
by hire car	**in macchina a noleggio**
by boat	**in barca / in nave**
by ferry	**in traghetto**
by bike	**in bicicletta**
on horseback	**a cavallo**
on foot	**a piedi**
timetable	**l'orario**
ticket	**il biglietto**
booking, reservation	**la prenotazione**

on-line booking	**la prenotazione per internet / on-line**
arrival	**l'arrivo**
departure	**la partenza**

Insight

Where English uses *by* with means of transport, Italian always uses in – so *by car* is in **macchina**, *by plane* is **in aereo**, etc. But *on foot* and *on horseback* are **a piedi** and **a cavallo**.

Useful verbs

to travel	**viaggiare**
to go	**andare**
to sail	**navigare / viaggiare per mare**
to fly	**volare / andare in aereo**
to drive	**viaggiare in macchina**
to tour	**fare un giro di / fare un viaggio in**
to arrive	**arrivare**
to leave	**partire**

Useful phrases

Can you help me, please?	**Mi può aiutare?/ Mi aiuti, per favore!**
I'm lost	**Mi sono perso**
How do I get to ...?	**Come posso andare a ...?**
What is the best way to go to ...?	**Mi sa indicare la strada migliore per ...?**
Is it far?	**È lontano?**
How far is it?	**Quanto è lontano?**
How long does it take?	**Quanto tempo ci vuole per andare?**

Expand your vocabulary by grouping words which have the same root: **viaggio** means *journey*; **viaggiare** *to travel*; **agenzia di viaggi** *travel agency*.

11.2 Travel by train

Core vocabulary

station	**la stazione**
station master	**il capostazione**
booking office	**la biglietteria / l'ufficio prenotazioni**
ticket machine	**la biglietteria automatica**
timetable	**l'orario**
ticket	**il biglietto**
single ticket	**il biglietto di andata**
return ticket	**il biglietto di andata e ritorno**

Train travel in Italy is very reasonably priced, and trains are very punctual; among other express trains are the various **Intercity** trains, **Pendolino** and **Eurostar**.

types of ticket	**tipi di biglietto**
child	**per bambino**
adult	**per adulto**
family	**offerta famiglie**
senior/pensioners	**per pensionati**
group	**di gruppo**
arrivals	**arrivi**
departures	**partenze**
indicator board	**il tabellone**
information	**informazioni** (f pl)
waiting room	**la sala d'attesa**
platform	**il marciapiede / binario**
subway / underpass	**il sottopassaggio**
stairs	**la scala**
lift	**l'ascensore** (m)
train	**il treno**
express	**l'espresso**
Inter-city	**l'intercity** (m)
local / slow	**il treno locale**

underground	**il metrò / la metropolitana**
coach	**la carrozza / vettura**
non-smoking	**per non fumatori**
first class	**di prima classe**
buffet	**il servizio ristoro**
personnel	**il personale**
guard	**il capotreno**
ticket inspector	**il controllore**
train driver	**il macchinista**
passenger	**il passeggero**
traveller	**il viaggiatore**
level crossing	**il passaggio a livello**
railway track	**la linea ferroviaria**
signals	**i segnali ferroviari**
luggage	**i bagagli**
suitcase	**la valigia**
left luggage	**il deposito bagagli**

Useful verbs

to book a ticket	**prenotare un biglietto**
to make a reservation	**fare una prenotazione**

Useful phrases

Do I have to change?	**Devo cambiare?**
Is the train on time?	**Il treno è / arriverà in orario?**
How late is the train?	**Con quanto ritardo arriva il treno?**
Will I miss the connection?	**Perderò la coincidenza?**
Is there a car park at the station?	**C'è un parcheggio alla stazione?**
Which platform does it leave from?	**Da quale binario parte il treno?**
Is this the train for ...?	**È il treno per ...?**
This is my place	**Questo posto è mio**
I have a reservation	**Ho fatto una prenotazione**
the underground / subway	**il metrò / la metropolitana**

the line	**la linea**
How often does it run?	**Ogni quanto c'è il treno?**
Which line do I need for ...?	**Quale linea devo prendere per ...?**

11.3 Travel by plane

Core vocabulary

At the airport **All'aeroporto**

car park	**il parcheggio**
departures	**le partenze**
check-in desk	**il check-in / banco accettazioni**
luggage search	**il controllo bagagli**
security check	**il controllo di sicurezza**

Which class?	**Quale classe?**
economy	**classe turistica**
business	**classe business**
first	**prima classe**
ticket	**il biglietto**
passport	**il passaporto**
visa	**il visto**
green card	**la carta verde**

departure lounge	**la sala partenze**
executive lounge	**la sala VIP**
information	**le informazioni** (f)
announcements	**gli annunci**
flight	**il volo**
gate	**l'uscita**
delay	**il ritardo**

On the plane **In aereo**

row	**la fila**
seat	**il posto**
window seat	**il posto vicino al finestrino**
aisle seat	**il posto vicino al corridoio**
seat belt	**la cintura di sicurezza**

life jacket	**il giubbotto di salvataggio**
emergency exit	**l'uscita di sicurezza**
overhead locker	**lo scomparto del bagaglio a mano**
toilet	**il gabinetto**
pilot	**il pilota**
steward	**lo steward**
stewardess	**la hostess**
Can I have ...?	**Mi dia ...**
earphones	**la cuffia**
a blanket	**una coperta**
a pillow	**un cuscino**
a glass of water	**un bicchiere d'acqua**

Landing **L'atterraggio**

arrivals	**arrivi**
baggage reclaim	**il ritiro bagagli**
customs	**la dogana**
duty	**il dazio**

Useful verbs

to leave / depart	**partire**
to take off	**decollare**
to fly	**volare**
to land	**atterrare**
to arrive	**arrivare**
to navigate	**navigare**
to put the seat back	**inclinare il sedile indietro**
to put the seat upright	**mettere il sedile in posizione verticale**
to stow the table	**chiudere il tavolino pieghevole**
to experience turbulence	**attraversare una zona di turbolenza dell'aria**

The plane is delayed	**L'aereo è in ritardo**
Your flight leaves from gate ...	**Il Suo volo parte dall'uscita numero ...**
Please will you return to your seats and fasten your seat-belts	**Si prega di tornare ai propri posti e allacciare la cintura di sicurezza**
We are flying at an altitude of ...	**Siamo a un'altezza di ...**
... and a speed of ...	**... e a una velocità di ...**
My luggage is missing	**I miei bagagli non ci sono**

11.4 Travel by car

Core vocabulary

car	**la macchina**
estate car	**la station wagon / l'auto modello familiare**
four wheel drive	**con trazione a quattro ruote motrici**
sports car	**l'automobile sportiva**
convertible	**l'auto decappottabile**
automatic	**l'automobile con cambio automatico**
2/4 doors	**con 2/4 portiere**
16 valves	**con 16 valvole**
the pedals	**i pedali**
accelerator	**l'acceleratore** (m)
brake	**il freno**
clutch	**il pedale della frizione**
the windscreen	**il parabrezza**
the gears	**le marce**
the gear lever	**la leva del cambio**
the steering wheel	**il volante**

the handbrake	**il freno a mano**
the indicators	**le frecce**
the lights	**le luci**
headlamps	**i fari / fanali**
side lights	**le luci di posizione**
on full	**con gli abbaglianti accesi**
on dipped	**con i fari abbassati / gli anabbaglianti**
the speedometer	**il tachimetro**
the mileometer	**il contachilometri**
the petrol gauge	**la spia della benzina**

The interior **L'interno**

seats	**i sedili**
safety belt	**la cintura di sicurezza**
leg room	**lo spazio per le gambe**
glove compartment	**il vano portaoggetti**
sunvisor	**l'aletta parasole**
wing mirror	**lo specchietto laterale esterno**
rear-view mirror	**lo specchietto retrovisore**
heating	**il riscaldamento**
air conditioning	**l'aria condizionata**

The wheels **Le ruote**

tyres	**le gomme / i pneumatici**
valve	**la valvola**
tyre pressure	**la pressione dei pneumatici**
jack	**il cric**
spare wheel	**la ruota di scorta**

The exterior **L'esterno**

boot	**il bagagliaio**
bumper	**il paraurti**
number plate	**la targa**
fog lights	**i fari antinebbia**
rear lights	**le luci posteriori**
exhaust	**il tubo di scappamento**
battery	**la batteria**
radiator	**il radiatore**

Getting technical **Aspetti tecnici**

ignition	**l'accensione** (f)
spark plug	**la candela**
water hose	**il manicotto dell'acqua**
oil pressure	**la pressione dell'olio**
fan belt	**la cinghia della ventola**
windscreen wiper	**il tergicristallo**
windscreen washer	**il lavacristallo**
warning light	**la spia luminosa**

Useful verbs

to drive	**guidare**
to put your lights on	**accendere le luci**
to turn your lights off	**spegnere le luci**
to put your indicator on	**mettere la freccia / segnalare**
to give way	**dare la precedenza**
to overtake	**sorpassare**

Useful phrases

You have left your lights on	**Ha lasciato le luci accese**
How do I move the seat?	**Come posso aggiustare il sedile?**

11.5 The road

Core vocabulary

a country road	**una strada di campagna**
a main road	**una strada principale**
a one-way road	**una strada a senso unico**
a dual carriageway	**una strada a doppia carreggiata**
a motorway	**un'autostrada**
a motorway lane	**una corsia dell'autostrada**
the inside lane	**la corsia di destra**

the outside lane	**la corsia di sinistra**
the central reservation	**la banchina spartitraffico**
the access road	**la strada d'accesso**
motorway access road	**il raccordo di entrata**

Most, but not all motorways in Italy are toll roads. It is a good idea to have enough change ready when you get to a **casello** *toll station*, though you can also pay with a credit card or by **telepass**, an electronic system which reads your number plate and charges the toll directly to your account.

the road surface is ...	**il fondo stradale è**
good/bad	**in buone / cattive condizioni**
smooth/uneven	**liscio / disuguale**
bumpy	**dissestato**
with potholes	**con buche**
the intersection / cross-roads	**l'incrocio**
T-junction	**l'incrocio a T**
the roundabout	**la rotatoria**
the bridge	**il ponte**
the toll bridge	**il ponte a pedaggio**
the level crossing	**il passaggio a livello**
traffic lights	**il semaforo**

Note that Italian traffic lights go from green (**luce verde**) to amber (**luce gialla**) to red (**luce rossa**), then straight back to green with no red+amber phase.

road works	**i lavori stradali**
emergency traffic lights	**il semaforo d'emergenza**
the diversion	**la deviazione**
road signs	**i cartelli stradali**
crawler lane	**la corsia riservata al traffico lento**
hard shoulder	**la corsia d'emergenza**
the speed limit	**il limite di velocità**
the speed camera	**il controllo elettronico di velocità**
traffic police	**la polizia stradale**

driving licence	**la patente di guida**
insurance	**l'assicurazione**
fine	**la multa**
garage (for repairs / service)	**l'autofficina**
petrol station	**la stazione di servizio / il benzinaio**
petrol	**la benzina**
diesel	**il diesel**
air	**l'aria**
water	**l'acqua**
oil	**l'olio**
oil change	**il cambio dell'olio**
emergency services	**i servizi di pronto intervento**
breakdown	**il guasto**

Useful verbs

to speed	**andare a velocità eccessiva**
to accelerate	**accelerare**
to slow down	**rallentare**
to brake	**frenare**
to break down	**avere un guasto**

Useful phrases

I have broken down	**La mia macchina è guasta**
The car is overheating	**La macchina si surriscalda**
The engine has stopped	**Il motore non funziona più / si è fermato**
I have a puncture	**Ho forato una gomma / Ho una gomma a terra**
The silencer has blown	**La marmitta è scoppiata**

TEST YOURSELF

Look at these groups of words and identify each group as 'trains', 'planes' or 'automobiles'. Then write down the English for the words.

1 il binario, la stazione, l'orario, il sottopassaggio, il treno
2 il check-in, il passaporto, il volo, classe business, il pilota
3 la macchina, le frecce, le luci, il parabrezza, il tachimetro
4 la spia della benzina, i pedali, il freno a mano, le gomme, la candela
5 le partenze, la cuffia, atterrare, il tavolino pieghevole, lo steward
6 il capotreno, i bagagli, l'espresso, il treno locale, il passaggio a livello
7 il servizio ristoro, i segnali ferroviari, l'intercity, la sala d'attesa, il macchinista
8 l'incrocio, la rotatoria, il semaforo, una strada a doppia carreggiata, la multa
9 decollare, attraversare una zona di turbolenza dell'aria, volare, il pilota, la fila
10 il paraurti, la targa, sorpassare, il cric, la ruota di scorta

Answers:
1 trains: platform, station, timetable, subway, train
2 planes: check-in, passport, flight, business class, pilot
3 automobiles: car, indicators/turn signals*, lights, windscreen/windshield*, speedometer/odometer
4 automobiles: fuel gauge/gas gauge*, pedals, handbrake/parking brake*, tyres/tires*, spark plug
5 planes: departures, headphones, to land, tray table, steward
6 trains: guard, luggage, express, local train, level crossing
7 trains: buffet, signals, intercity, waiting room, timetable, train driver
8 automobiles: crossroads, roundabout/traffic circle*, traffic lights/stop light*, dual carriageway/four-lane highway*, fine
9 planes: to take off, to experience turbulence, to fly, pilot, row
10 automobiles: bumper, number plate/license plate*, to overtake, jack, spare wheel
* US.

12

Tourism

12.1 Where to go

Core vocabulary

the tourism industry	l'industria turistica, il turismo
travel agency	l'agenzia di viaggi
a brochure	un opusculo / dépliant
the tourist	il/la turista
an excursion	un'escursione, una gita
a tour	un giro
a coach trip	un'escursione in pullman
a guided visit	una visita guidata
a cruise	una crociera
holiday resort	il luogo di villeggiatura
seaside	la spiaggia / il mare
sea sand and sun	il mare, la sabbia e il sole
mountains and lakes	le montagne e i laghi
countryside	la campagna
adventure holidays	le vacanze di avventure
winter sports	gli sport invernali
outdoor pursuits	le attività all'aperto

to go on holiday	**andare in vacanza / prendere le ferie**
to go on summer holiday	**prendere le vacanze estive**
national holiday	**le feste civili**

Expand your vocabulary by grouping words which have the same root, e.g. **turista**, **turismo** and **turistico**.

12.2 What to take

Core vocabulary

luggage	**i bagagli**
suitcase	**la valigia**
travel bag	**la borsa da viaggio**
overnight bag	**la borsa da viaggio / la ventiquattrore**
rucksack	**lo zaino**
hand luggage	**il bagaglio a mano**
passport	**il passaporto**
visa	**il visto**
tickets	**i biglietti**
insurance	**l'assicurazione**
driving licence	**la patente di guida**
credit card	**la carta di credito**
currency	**la valuta estera**
traveller's cheque	**il traveller's cheque**
emergency phone number	**il numero di telefono d'emergenza**
laptop	**il laptop**
mobile phone	**il telefonino**
sponge bag	**il nécessaire**
toilet bag	**il nécessaire da toilette**
soap	**il sapone**
toothbrush	**lo spazzolino da denti**

toothpaste	**il dentifricio**
razor	**il rasoio**
electric razor	**il rasoio elettrico**
nail scissors	**le forbicine per le unghie**
tweezers	**le pinzette**
shampoo	**lo shampoo**
conditioner	**il balsamo**
hairbrush	**la spazzola per capelli**
comb	**il pettine**
face cream	**la crema per il viso**
hand cream	**la crema per le mani**
cleanser	**il detergente**
moisturizer	**il prodotto idratante**
sun cream	**la crema solare**
waterproof sun cream	**la crema solare impermeabile**
after sun cream	**la crema doposole**
factor 10	**la crema solare con fattore di protezione 10**

Useful verbs

to pack	**fare le valigie / i bagagli**
to unpack	**disfare le valigie / i bagagli**
to fold	**piegare**
to hang up	**appendere**
to wash	**lavare**
to dry clean	**lavare a secco**
to mend	**rammendare / aggiustare / riparare**
to press / iron	**stirare**

Useful phrases

I have lost my luggage	**Ho perso i miei bagagli**
I can't find ...	**Non trovo ...**
Have you got a ...?	**Ha un(a) ...?**
Where can I get a ...?	**Dove posso trovare un(a) ...?**
Where is the nearest ...?	**Dove sta il/la .... più vicino?**

12.3 Where to stay

Core vocabulary

accommodation	**l'alloggio**
two-star hotel	**un albergo a due stelle**
three-star hotel	**un albergo a tre stelle**
luxury hotel	**un albergo di lusso**
inn	**la locanda**
bed and breakfast	**la pensione familiare**
holiday house / home	**la casa di villeggiatura**
youth hostel	**l'ostello della gioventù**
camp site	**il campeggio**
caravan site	**il campeggio per roulotte**
the entrance	**l'entrata / l'ingresso**
the reception	**la reception**
the night porter	**il portiere di notte**
the manager	**il direttore / gerente**
the staff	**il personale**
the porter	**il portiere**
a single room	**una camera singola**
a room with double bed	**una (camera) matrimoniale**
a twin bedded room	**una (camera) doppia**
a family room	**una camera familiare**
with shower	**con doccia**
with bathroom	**con bagno**
with toilet	**con gabinetto**
with phone	**con telefono**
with television	**con televisione**
with Internet connection	**con connessione a Internet**
with a balcony	**con balcone**
with a sea view	**con vista sul mare**
with air conditioning	**con aria condizionata**
stairs	**la scala**
lift	**l'ascensore**
restaurant	**il ristorante**
fitness room	**la palestra per esercizi di fitness**

pool	la piscina
hot tub	la vasca per idromassaggio
the bill	il conto

Useful phrases

Have you got anything ...?	Ha qualcosa di ...?
bigger / smaller	più grande / piccolo
cheaper / better	meno caro / migliore
quieter	più tranquillo
a non-smoking room	una camera per non fumatori
It is too noisy	È troppo rumoroso
The shower doesn't work	Non funziona la doccia
There is no hot water	Non c'è acqua calda
There is no plug in the sink	Non c'è il tappo nel lavandino
Can I have another towel?	Posso avere un altro asciugamano?
more coat hangers?	altre grucce?
the iron?	il ferro da stiro?

12.4 Camping and caravanning

Core vocabulary

camp site	il campeggio
caravan	la roulotte
camper van	il camper
trailer	il rimorchio
tent	la tenda
frame tent	la tenda familiare
site	il posto
a flat site	un posto piano
a shady site	un posto ombreggiato
facilities	le attrezzature
electricity	l'elettricità / la corrente
water	l'acqua
running water	l'acqua corrente

drinking water	**l'acqua potabile**
water tap	**il rubinetto dell'acqua**
power socket	**la presa di corrente**
washrooms / toilets	**i gabinetti**
showers	**le docce**
washbasins	**i lavandini**
hairdryers	**gli asciugacapelli**
cooking area	**la cucina**
gas rings	**i fornelli a gas**
washing up sinks	**i lavelli**
washing machines	**le lavatrici**
clothes driers	**le asciugatrici / asciugabiancheria**
drying area	**la zona per asciugare i panni**
restaurant	**il ristorante**
bar	**il bar**
shop	**il negozio**
swimming pool	**la piscina**
paddling pool	**la piscina per bambini**
children's play area	**il campo giochi per bambini**
swings	**l'altalena**
slide	**lo scivolo**
roundabout	**la giostra**
tent	**la tenda**
tent pegs	**i picchetti (da tenda)**
tent pole	**il palo da tenda**
guy ropes	**i tiranti / cavi**
ground-sheet	**il telone impermeabile**
sleeping bag	**il sacco a pelo**
torch	**la torcia elettrica**
blanket	**la coperta**
gas cooker	**la cucina a gas**
gas bottle	**la bombola del gas**

Useful verbs

to tow	**rimorchiare**
to park	**parcheggiare**

to put up	**montare**
to take down	**smontare**
to hook up (connect)	**collegare**
to get wet	**bagnarsi**
to wash / do the washing	**fare il bucato**
to dry	**asciugare**

Useful phrases

Can you help me?	**Mi può aiutare?**
I don't understand how the ... works	**Non capisco come funziona il/ la ...**
Where is the ...?	**Dove sta il/la ...?**
Is there electricity / water / shade?	**C'è elettricità / acqua / ombra?**
Do you have ...?	**Ha ...?**
When is the shop open?	**A che ora apre il negozio?**
Where can I get ...?	**Dove posso trovare ...?**

12.5 What are you going to do?

Core vocabulary

an activity holiday	**delle vacanze con attività programmate**
we want to go ...	**vogliamo andare a fare ...**
swimming	**il nuoto**
diving	**i tuffi**
water skiing	**lo sci nautico**
surfing	**il surf**
walking	**la camminata**
hiking	**la gita a piedi**
climbing	**l'alpinismo**
gliding	**il volo a vela**
paragliding	**il volo col paracadute**
hanggliding	**il volo col deltaplano**
do sport	**fare dello sport**
play tennis	**giocare a tennis**

| play volleyball | **giocare a pallavolo** |
| go bike riding | **fare ciclismo** |

we want to see	**vogliamo vedere**
monuments / sights	**i monumenti**
castles	**i castelli**
archeological sites	**i siti archeologici**
ancient monuments	**i monumenti antichi**
historic buildings	**gli edifici storici**
the scenery	**il paesaggio**
animals	**gli animali**

we want ...	**vogliamo ...**
to have a good time	**divertirci***
to have a rest	**riposarci***
to relax	**rilassarci***
sun, sea and sand	**sole, mare e sabbia**
to do nothing	**non fare niente**
to be waited on	**essere serviti**

*These expressions are reflexive, and we have put the pronoun into the **ci** form, which is what you will need after **vogliamo**.

In winter I like to go ...	**d'inverno mi piace ...**
skiing	**andare a sciare**
snowboarding	**fare lo snowboard**
sledging	**andare in slitta**
ice skating	**fare il pattinaggio sul ghiaccio**
to find some sun	**trovare il sole**

Useful phrases

What is there to see / do?	**Che c'è da vedere / fare?**
Is it suitable for ...?	**È adatto per ...?**
older people	**gli anziani**
younger people	**i giovani**
children	**i bambini**

12.6 On the beach

Core vocabulary

sea	il mare
coast	la costa
beach	la spiaggia
bay	la baia
shore	la riva
sand	la sabbia
rocks	le rocce
rock pools	le pozze d'acqua
sea shells	le conchiglie
tide	la marea
waves	le onde
private / public beach	la spiaggia privata / pubblica
wind break	il frangivento
shelter	il rifugio
parasol	il parasole
lounger	il lettino da spiaggia
deck chair	la sedia a sdraio
air mattress	il materassino gonfiabile

shower	**la doccia**
towel	**l'asciugamano**
swimming costume	**il costume da bagno**
trunks	**i calzoncini da bagno**
bikini	**il bikini**
suntan lotion	**l'olio solare**
total screen / sunblock	**il filtro solare**
sun glasses	**gli occhiali da sole**
rubber ring	**la ciambella**
arm bands	**i braccioli per bambini**
sandcastle	**il castello di sabbia**
bucket	**il secchio**
spade	**la paletta**
kite	**l'aquilone**
snorkel	**il respiratore subacqueo / boccaglio**
flippers	**le pinne**
wet suit	**la muta da subacqueo**
dry suit	**la sottomuta**
inflatable	**gonfiabile**
hand/foot pump	**la pompa a mano / a pedale**
surf board	**il surf**
wind surfer	**il windsurfista**
jetski	**la moto acquatica**
waterski	**lo sci nautico**
fish	**il pesce**
shells	**le conchiglie**
octopus	**il polpo**
squid	**il calamaro**
mussels	**le cozze**
scallops	**le cappe sante**
shrimps	**i gamberetti**
jelly fish	**la medusa**

Useful verbs

to snorkel	**nuotare con il boccaglio**
to sunbathe	**prendere il sole**
to relax	**rilassarsi**
to play	**giocare**
to dig	**scavare**
to dive	**tuffarsi**
to sting	**pizzicare / pungere**
to waterski	**praticare lo sci nautico**

Useful phrases

The tide is in / out	**La marea è alta / bassa**
It is safe for bathing / swimming	**Non è pericoloso bagnarsi / nuotare**
I have been stung by a jelly fish	**Mi ha pizzicato una medusa**
He/She is out of her depth	**Lui/Lei non tocca**
He/She can't swim	**Lui/Lei non sa nuotare**
He/She needs help	**Ha bisogno di aiuto**
Help!	**Aiuto!**

12.7 At sea

Core vocabulary

canoe	**la canoa**
jetski	**la moto acquatica**
motor boat	**il motoscafo**
outboard (motor)	**il (motore) fuoribordo**
RIB (rigid inflatable boat)	**il gommone a chiglia rigida**
rubber dinghy	**il gommone**
rowing boat	**la barca a remi**
sailing dinghy	**la deriva**
surf board	**il surf**
waterski	**lo sci nautico**
windsurfer	**il windsurfista**
yacht	**il panfilo da diporto**

emergency services	i servizi di pronto intervento
MAYDAY	MAYDAY
SOS	SOS
lifeboat (from shore)	la lancia di salvataggio
lifeboat (from ship)	la scialuppa di salvataggio
life jacket	il giubbotto di salvataggio
lifeguard	il bagnino
flare	il segnale luminoso
weather forecast	le previsioni del tempo
the sea is	il mare è
calm	calmo
rough	mosso
wind force	la forza del vento
gale force wind	il vento di bufera
rain	la pioggia
poor / good visibility	poca / buona visibilità
fog	la nebbia
equipment	l'attrezzatura
compass	la bussola
GPS (global satellite positioning)	il navigatore GPS
sails	le vele
hull	lo scafo
cabin	la cabina
berth	la cuccetta
wheel	il timone
harbour	il porto
port	il porto
lighthouse	il faro
port	(a) babordo
starboard	(a) tribordo
mooring	l'ormeggio
buoy	la boa
chain	la catena
anchor	l'ancora

Useful verbs

to sail	**navigare**
to navigate	**navigare**
to steer	**governare / dirigere**
to tie up / moor	**ormeggiare**
to anchor	**ancorare**
to rescue	**salvare**
to be rescued	**essere salvato/a**

12.8 The great outdoors

Core vocabulary

rucksack	**lo zaino**
sleeping bag	**il sacco a pelo**
ground mat / mattress	**il materassino**
torch	**la torcia elettrica**
penknife	**il temperino**
compass	**la bussola**
map	**la mappa**
water bottle	**la borraccia**
camping stove	**il fornelletto a gas**
matches	**i fiammiferi**
lighter	**l'accendino**
gas container	**la bombola del gas**
billycan (for cooking on stove)	**il pentolino**
bowl	**la scodella / coppetta**
knife / fork / spoon	**il coltello / la forchetta / il cucchiaio**
plate	**il piatto**
mug	**il tazzone**
emergency rations	**le razioni di riserva**
dried food	**alimenti liofilizzati / disidratati**
dried fruit / nuts	**la frutta secca**
walnuts, hazelnuts, almonds	**le noci, le nocciole, le mandorle**
chocolate	**il cioccolato**

transceiver (for snow rescue)	**il ricetrasmettitore**
mobile phone	**il telefonino**
batteries	**le pile / la batteria**
charger	**il carica-batterie**
plug	**la spina**
waterproofs	**gli indumenti impermeabili**
spare clothing	**i vestiti di scorta**
rope	**la corda**
climbing harness	**l'imbracatura da alpinismo**
climbing gear	**l'attrezzatura da alpinismo**
crampons	**i ramponi**
boots	**gli stivali**
ice axe	**la piccozza da ghiaccio**

Useful phrases

I have got ... sore feet	**Mi fanno male ... i piedi**
Have you got ...	**Hai / ha ...?**
spare socks	**dei calzini di scorta**
blisters	**le vesciche**
plasters	**dei cerotti**
antiseptic cream	**della pomata antisettica**
insect repellent	**l'insettifugo**
Have you got something for ...?	**Ha qualche cosa per ...?**
I have been stung by a	**Mi ha punto una**
wasp / bee	**vespa / un'ape**
I have been bitten by ...	**Mi ha morso ...**
a mosquito	**una zanzara**
a snake	**un serpente**
a dog	**un cane**

Insight

To say something nasty has happened to you, you often use a phrase beginning with **Mi ...** In this context, **mi** can either just mean *me* (**mi ha punto una vespa, mi ha pizzicato una medusa**, *a wasp/jellyfish has stung me*) or have the sense of *to me* (**mi fanno male i piedi** – literally, *my feet are doing harm to me*).

TEST YOURSELF

Look at the Italian for each of these English words or phrases and pick **a**, **b** or **c** as appropriate, to complete each expression.

1 moisturizer: il prodotto **a** idratante **b** impermeabile **c** per capelli
2 hairbrush: la spazzola per **a** denti **b** bagagli **c** capelli
3 to pack: fare le **a** lavandino **b** stelle **c** valigie
4 to go on holiday: prendere le **a** capelli **b** ferie **c** gerente
5 hot tub / jacuzzi: La vasca per **a** corrente **b** idromassaggio **c** roulotte
6 caravan site: il campeggio per **a** roulotte **b** grucce **c** lavandini
7 arm bands: i braccioli per **a** moglie **b** nonne **c** bambini
8 lounger: il lettino da **a** ghiaccio **b** spiaggia **c** boccaglio
9 weather forecast: le previsioni del **a** tempo **b** cucchiaio **c** bufera
10 I have been stung by **a** jellyfish: mi ha pizzicato una a riva **b** medusa **c** boa

Answers: 1a, 2c, 3c, 4b, 5b, 6a, 7c, 8b, 9a, 10b

13

Body and health

13.1 The face

Core vocabulary

head	**la testa**
face	**la faccia / il viso**
hair	**i capelli**
forehead	**la fronte**
ears	**le orecchie**
eyes	**gli occhi**
eyebrows	**le sopracciglia**
eyelashes	**le ciglia**
nose	**il naso**
nostrils	**le narici**
cheeks	**le guance**
chin	**il mento**
mouth	**la bocca**
lips	**le labbra**
tongue	**la lingua**
teeth	**i denti**
neck	**il collo**
He has a beard	**ha la barba**
a moustache	**i baffi**
He / she wears glasses	**porta gli occhiali**

contact lenses	**le lenti a contatto**
I am short/long-sighted	**sono miope / presbite**

Toiletries **Articoli di toeletta**

shampoo	**lo shampoo**
conditioner	**il balsamo**
face cream	**la crema per il viso**
moisturizer	**la crema idratante**
face pack	**la maschera di bellezza**
lip salve	**il burro di cacao**
shaving cream	**la crema da barba**
shaving brush	**il pennello da barba**
razor	**il rasoio**
electric razor	**il rasoio elettrico**
after shave lotion	**il dopobarba**
make-up	**i cosmetici**
mascara	**il mascara**
lipstick	**il rossetto**
eye shadow	**l'ombretto**
powder	**la cipria**

Useful verbs

to feel	**sentire**
to hear	**sentire / udire**
to see	**vedere**
to smell	**sentire odore di**
to taste	**gustare / sentire il sapore di**
to wink	**fare l'occhiolino**
to sleep	**dormire**
to smile	**sorridere**
to laugh	**ridere**
to talk	**parlare**
to shout	**gridare**
to cry	**piangere**
to snore	**russare**
to hiccup	**avere il singhiozzo**
to cough	**tossire**

Useful phrases

to have a facial	**farsi fare un trattamento di bellezza per il viso**
to have your hair done	**andare dal parrucchiere**
to have a nose job	**essere operato al naso**
to have plastic surgery	**subire la chirurgia plastica**
to have wrinkles	**avere le rughe**
to have a nice smile	**avere un bel sorriso**

13.2 The body

Core vocabulary

body	**il corpo**
shoulders	**le spalle**
back	**la schiena**
arms	**le braccia**
elbows	**i gomiti**
wrist	**il polso**
hands	**le mani**
fingers	**le dita**
thumb	**il pollice**
fingernails	**le unghie**
front	**il davanti**
side	**il fianco**
chest	**il petto**

breasts	**i seni**
nipples	**i capezzoli**
waist	**la vita**
hips	**i fianchi**
abdomen	**l'addome**
bottom	**il sedere**
sexual organs	**gli organi sessuali**
penis	**il pene**
balls	**i coglioni**
vagina	**la vagina**
legs	**le gambe**
thighs	**le cosce**
knees	**le ginocchia**
calves	**i polpacci**
ankle	**la caviglia**
foot	**il piede**
toes	**le dita del piede**
arch	**l'arco**
heel	**il tallone**
internal organs	**gli organi interni**
brain	**il cervello**
stomach	**lo stomaco**
belly	**la pancia**
throat	**la gola**
lungs	**i polmoni**
kidneys	**i reni**
heart	**il cuore**
blood	**il sangue**
veins	**le vene**
arteries	**le arterie**
a blood transfusion	**una trasfusione di sangue**
a blood donor	**un donatore di sangue**
my blood type	**il mio gruppo sanguigno**
intestines	**gli intestini**
skeleton	**lo scheletro**
bones	**le ossa**

joints	le articolazioni
nervous system	il sistema nervoso
nerves	i nervi
circulation	la circolazione
breathing	la respirazione
digestion	la digestione

Useful verbs

to feel	sentire
to touch	toccare
to stroke	accarezzare
to massage	massaggiare
to hold	tenere
to embrace	abbracciarsi
to kiss	baciarsi
to make love	fare l'amore
to kick	dar calci (a)
to walk	camminare
to run	correre
to jump	saltare

13.3 I need a doctor

Core vocabulary

doctor	il medico / dottore
appointment	l'appuntamento
surgery	l'ambulatorio
I have a pain ...	ho mal di ...
it hurts / they hurt	mi fa male / mi fanno male
I don't feel well	non mi sento bene
I can't sleep / eat / walk ...	non posso dormire / mangiare / camminare
I want to go to the toilet	voglio andare al gabinetto / al bagno
I feel sick	mi sento male / ho la nausea

I feel dizzy	**mi gira la testa**
I have got spots	**ho dei foruncoli**
I have been bitten / stung	**sono stato morsicato / punto**
I have a headache	**ho mal di testa**
toothache	**mal di denti**
earache	**mal d'orecchi**
a nose bleed	**un'emorragia nasale**
my eyes are sore	**mi fanno male gli occhi**
I have stomach-ache	**ho mal di stomaco**
heart burn	**il bruciore di stomaco**
indigestion	**l'indigestione**
high/low blood pressure	**la pressione alta/bassa**
my foot / hand / leg hurts	**mi fa male il piede / la mano / la gamba**

Ailments **Disturbi e malattie**

a cold	**un raffreddore**
flu (influenza)	**l'influenza**
measles	**il morbillo**
mumps	**gli orecchioni**
German measles	**la rosolia**
tonsillitis	**la tonsillite**
a cough	**una tosse**
sore throat	**un mal di gola**
indigestion	**la cattiva digestione / l'indigestione**
hypertension	**l'ipertensione**
constipation	**la stitichezza**
diarrhoea	**la diarrea**
polio	**la polio(mielite)**
hepatitis	**l'epatite** *(f)*
rabies	**la rabbia / l'idrofobia**
typhoid	**la febbre tifoidea**
cholera	**il colera**
yellow fever	**la febbre gialla**
malaria	**la malaria**
cancer	**il cancro**
multiple sclerosis	**la sclerosi a placche**

I am allergic to	**sono allergico**
penicillin	**alla penicillina**
nuts	**alle noci**
animals	**agli animali**
I have hay fever	**ho il raffreddore da fieno**
asthma	**l'asma**
He needs an inhaler	**Lui ha bisogno di un inalatore**
She is handicapped	**Lei è handicappata**
paraplegic	**paraplegico**
She has her period	**Lei ha le mestruazioni**

Treatment Cure

an injection / a jab for	**un'iniezione per**
immunization	**l'immunizzazione**
innoculation	**l'inoculazione**
medicine	**la medicina**
pills	**le pillole**
pain relief	**il sollievo al dolore**
vitamin supplements	**i supplementi vitaminici**
cure	**la cura**
homeopathic remedy	**il rimedio omeopatico**
exercise	**l'esercizio**
physiotherapy	**la fisioterapia**
rest	**il riposo**
go to bed	**va' / vada al letto**
take more exercise	**fa' / faccia del movimento**
eat less	**mangia / mangi di meno**

13.4 At the hospital

Core vocabulary

hospital	**l'ospedale**
department	**il dipartimento / reparto**
emergency	**l'emergenza / urgenza**
doctor	**il medico**

nurse	**l'infermiera / l'infermiere**
ward	**la corsia / il reparto**
bed	**il letto**
a health certificate	**un certificato della salute**
an examination	**una visita**
an x-ray	**una radiografia**
radiation	**la radiazione**
I have broken my leg / ankle / wrist ...	**mi sono rotto la gamba / la caviglia / il polso**
plaster	**il gesso**
crutches	**le stampelle / grucce**
walking stick	**il bastone per camminare**
wheel chair	**la sedia a rotelle**
anaesthetic	**l'anestetico**
surgery (medical procedure)	**la chirurgia**
surgery (place)	**l'ambulatorio**
operation	**l'operazione / intervento chirurgico**
operating theatre	**la sala operatoria**
family planning	**la pianificazione familiare**
contraception	**la contraccezione**
condom	**il preservativo / profilattico**
the coil	**la spirale**
the pill	**la pillola**
the morning-after pill	**la pillola del giorno dopo**
vasectomy	**la vasectomia**

Insight

The ending **-zione** on an Italian word corresponds to the English endings *-tion* or *-sion*. This means that you have a very good chance of guessing the word correctly: **attenzione, tensione, immunizzazione, inoculazione,** etc.

TEST YOURSELF

Sort the ailments from the body parts. Then write the English for each word.

1 un rafreddore
2 la stitichezza
3 le labbra
4 la rabbia
5 i polmoni
6 mal di testa
7 la testa
8 l'epatite
9 i reni
10 le ginocchia

Answers:
Ailments: 1 a cold; 2 constipation; 4 rabies; 6 a headache; 8 hepatitis
Body parts: 3 lips; 5 lungs; 7 head; 9 kidneys; 10 knees

14

The world

14.1 Countries

Core vocabulary

the world	**il mondo**
the earth	**la terra**
the globe	**il globo**
the atlas	**l'atlante**
the continents	**i continenti**
Africa	**l'Africa**
America	**l'America**
North America	**l'America del Nord**
South America	**l'America del Sud**
Asia	**l'Asia**
Australia	**l'Australia**
Europe	**l'Europa**
the Arctic region	**l'Artide**
the Antarctic	**l'Antartide**
the Middle East	**il Medio Oriente**
the Far East	**l'Estremo Oriente**
the Pacific rim	**la Costa del Pacifico**
Indo-China	**l'Indocina**
India	**l'India**
China	**la Cina**

Japan	il Giappone
Indonesia	l'Indonesia
Australasia	Australia, Nuova Zelanda e Papua Nuova Guinea
New Zealand	la Nuova Zelanda
the Pacific Islands	le Isole del Pacifico

14.2 The countries of Europe

Core vocabulary

Europe	l'Europa
Scandinavia	la Scandinavia
Denmark	la Danimarca
Finland	la Finlandia
Norway	la Norvegia
Sweden	la Svezia
Iceland	l'Islanda
The Low Countries	i Paesi Bassi
Belgium	il Belgio
Holland	l'Olanda
Luxembourg	il Lussemburgo
the Iberian peninsula	la Penisola Iberica
Spain	la Spagna
Portugal	il Portogallo
the United Kingdom	il Regno Unito
England	l'Inghilterra
Scotland	la Scozia
Northern Ireland	l'Irlanda del Nord
Wales	il Galles
Greece	la Grecia
Turkey	la Turchia
Germany	la Germania
Poland	la Polonia
France	la Francia
Ireland	l'Irlanda
Austria	l'Austria
Italy	l'Italia

the Czech Republic	**la Repubblica Ceca**
Hungary	**l'Ungheria**
Slovakia	**la Slovacchia**
Switzerland	**la Svizzera**
European Union	**l'Unione Europea**
European Parliament	**il Parlamento Europeo**
Common Market	**il Mercato Comune**
Member of the European Parliament	**l'eurodeputato**
common agricultural policy	**la Politica Agricola Comune**
euro	**l'euro**
European institutions	**le istituzioni europee**
European Bank	**la Banca Europea**

14.3 The high seas

The points of the compass **I punti cardinali**

north, north-est, north-west	**nord, nord-est, nord-ovest**
south, south-east, south-west	**sud, sud-est, sud-ovest**
east	**est**
west	**ovest**
the compass	**la bussola**

The oceans and the seas **Gli oceani e i mari**

the Atlantic	**l'Atlantico**
the Indian	**l'Oceano Indiano**
the Pacific	**il Pacifico**
the Arctic	**l'Artico**
the Antartic	**l'Antartico**
the Mediterranean	**il Mediterraneo**
the North Sea	**il mare del Nord**
the Baltic	**il (mar) Baltico**
the Red Sea	**il mar Rosso**
the English Channel	**il Canale della Manica**
Ligurian Sea	**il mar Ligure**
Tyrrhenian Sea	**il mar Tirreno**
Adriatic Sea	**il mar Adriatico**

Ionian Sea	**il mar Ionio**
Bay of Naples / Salerno	**il Golfo di Napoli / Salerno**
Gulf of Genova / Taranto	**il Golfo di Genova / Taranto**
Straits of Messina	**lo stretto di Messina**
Sicily	**la Sicilia**
Sardinia	**la Sardegna**
Elba	**l'isola d'Elba**
navigation	**la navigazione**
longitude	**la longitudine**
latitude	**la latitudine**
equator	**l'equatore**
northern hemisphere	**l'emisfero settentrionale**
southern hemisphere	**l'emisfero australe**
tropics	**i tropici**
bay	**la baia**
island	**l'isola**
peninsula	**la penisola**
canal	**il canale**
Suez canal	**il canale di Suez**
Panama canal	**il canale di Panama**
straits	**lo stretto**
currents	**le correnti**
tides	**le maree**
ferry	**il traghetto**
liner	**il transatlantico**
cruise ship	**la nave da crociera**
tanker	**la petroliera**
container ship	**la nave portacontainer**
hazards	**i pericoli**
icebergs	**gli iceberg**
shipping	**la navigazione**
shipping forecast	**il meteo per la navigazione marittima**
storms	**le tempeste / burrasche**
gales	**i venti forti / le burrasche**

gale force (10)	**il vento forza 10**
rough seas	**i mari molto mossi**
calm seas	**i mari calmi**

Useful verbs

to board	**salire a bordo (di)**
to embark	**imbarcarsi**
to disembark	**sbarcare**

___

14.4 The weather forecast

Core vocabulary

rain	**la pioggia**
snow	**la neve**
wind	**il vento**
fog	**la nebbia**
sun	**il sole**
hail	**la grandine**
sleet	**il nevischio**
thunderstorm	**il temporale**
thunder	**il tuono**
lightening	**il fulmine / lampo**

What's the weather like?	**Che tempo fa?**
It is … raining	**piove / sta piovendo**
snowing	**nevica / sta nevicando**
cloudy	**è nuvoloso**
overcast	**è coperto**
rainy	**è piovoso**
wet / damp / humid	**è umido**
sunny	**c'è il sole**
windy	**c'è vento**
mild	**non fa freddo**
a dry day	**è un giorno senza pioggia**

It is warm, hot	**fa caldo, molto caldo**
cold	**fa freddo**
good weather	**fa bel tempo**
bad weather	**fa brutto tempo**
yesterday	**ieri**
today	**oggi**
tomorrow	**domani**
over the next few days	**nel corso dei prossimi giorni**
the weather is getting worse	**il tempo sta peggiorando**
improving	**migliorando**

Insight

You will need to pay attention to the phrases for describing the weather, because they are not quite like English. Most weather expressions in English are constructed along the lines of *it's ...ing*, but only some are like this in Italian. There are five basic types of phrase:

Simple verb: **piove/nevica**

Verb and gerund: **sta piovendo/nevicando**

Verb *to be* + adjective: **è umido/coperto** etc.

C'è + noun: **c'è il sole/c'è vento** etc.

Fa + adjective: **fa freddo/caldo** etc.

You can expect **Si può prevedere**

light / strong winds	**venti leggeri / forti**
rain / snow	**pioggia / neve**
clouds	**nuvole**
gusts of wind	**raffiche di vento**
gales	**venti forti / bufere**
storms	**tempeste / burrasche**
heavy showers	**rovesci / acquazzoni**
floods	**inondazioni**
sunny intervals	**intervalli di sole**
bright periods	**intervalli sereni**
prolonged spells of rain	**periodi prolungati di pioggia**
morning mist	**nebbiolina mattuttina**
fog patches	**banchi di nebbia**
frost	**gelo / brina**

| dangerous driving conditions | **condizioni delle strade pericolose per la guida** |
| risk of flooding | **rischio di inondazioni** |

The temperature **La temperatura**

degrees	**gradi**
Celsius/Centigrade	**Celsius / centigrado**
Fahrenheit	**Fahrenheit**
the temperature is rising / falling	**la temperatura sale / si abbassa**
maximum	**massimo**
minimum	**minimo**

Radio weather forecast

Le previsioni meteorologiche per domani: nella parte nord della regione cielo molto nuvoloso e pioggia intermittente, venti molto deboli. Il cielo sarà sereno o poco nuvoloso sulla parte meridionale, ma farà più freddo, con venti inizialmente deboli da nordest, ma di pomeriggio venti più forti, mari da poco mosso a mosso, temperature minime 5, massime 15. Dopo domani arriveranno dei temporali e venti molto forti, forza 5 a 6.

Newspaper weather forecast

venerdì 21 marzo

Nord: parzialmente nuvoloso al mattino per nubi alte e stratiformi; banchi di nebbia al mattino sulla pianura; aumento della nuvolosità durante la giornata sull'estremo settore occidentale, con possibilità di locali piogge in serata. Centro: sereno o poco nuvoloso. Locali banchi di nebbia al primo mattino nelle vallate. Sud: poco nuvoloso con locali annuvolamenti più estesi nel corso della giornata sulle zone a ridosso dei rilievi. Temperature: senza variazioni di rilievo. Venti: deboli nord-orientali con locali rinforzi sulle zone adriatiche. Mari: poco mossi; localmente mosso l'Adriatico e lo Ionio.

TEST YOURSELF

Match the countries or regions with the oceans that they are associated with.

1	la Grecia	a	lo Stretto di Messina
2	la Svezia	b	il mar Rosso
3	l'Inghilterra	c	il mare del Nord
4	l'Italia	d	l'Oceano Indiano
5	il Giappone	e	il mar Tirreno
6	il Belgio	f	il mar Baltico
7	l'Islanda	g	il mar Adriatico
8	l'India	h	l'Atlantico
9	la Sicilia	i	l Pacifico
10	il Medio Oriente	j	il Canale della Manica

Answers: 1g, 2f, 3j, 4e, 5i, 6c, 7h, 8d, 9a, 10b

15

Government and society

15.1 Politics and government

Core vocabulary

government	**il governo**
democracy	**la democrazia**
rule of law	**il principio di legalità**
dictatorship	**la dittatura**
monarchy	**la monarchia**
UK's Parliamentary Monarchy	**la monarchia parlamentare del Regno Unito**
Italy's Republican Democracy	**la democrazia repubblicana d'Italia**

A brief overview of Italy's current political situation
Una visione d'insieme della situazione politica d'Italia
Italy's democratic state is a fairly typical republic, in that there are
two parliamentary bodies – the House of Deputies and the Senate,
both consisting of elected members; unusually, perhaps, Italy has
both a President and a Prime Minister. An experienced politician
can be elected to the role of president, but then rarely becomes
involved directly in politics, having more of a figurehead role as
Head of State. The Prime Minister, on the other hand, is the head
of the government.

Italy has several main political parties, whose complex relationships have formed the many and usually short-lived governments of the last 60 years.

Democrazia Cristiana, which has most often formed the government, stands for conservative Christian values, a strong state, security and European commitment;

Partito Comunista Italiano, once the largest communist party in Europe and very influential, is now in decline.

Partito Socialista Italiano is a traditional Socialist party, standing for social justice and equality, but never ranking higher than third place.

Lega Nord was formed in 1989 to foster the interests of the prosperous north over the poorer south, and seeking independence from the rest of Italy.

In 2003, the Italian Royal Family, expelled from Italy when the Republic was formed in 1946 after World War II, was at long last allowed to visit Italy.

the Head of State	**il Capo dello Stato**
the President	**il Presidente**
the Prime Minister	**il Primo Ministro**
the King	**il Re**
the Queen	**la Regina**
the Royal Family	**la Famiglia Reale**
the Prince	**il Principe**
the Princess	**la Principessa**
to appoint one's government	**nominare il governo**
cabinet	**il Consiglio dei Ministri**
to appoint one's cabinet	**nominare il Consiglio dei Ministri**
the Minister of the Interior	**il Ministro degli Interni**
the Defence Minister	**il Ministro della Difesa**
the Chancellor of the Exchequer	**il Ministro del Tesoro**
the Justice Minister	**il Ministro della Giustizia**

parliament	**il parlamento**
chamber	**la camera**
Lower House (Italian Parliament)	**la Camera dei Deputati**
Upper House (Italian Parliament)	**il Senato**
member of lower house	**il deputato**
member of the higher chamber	**il senatore**
ministry	**il ministero**
Foreign Office	**il Ministero degli Esteri**
Home Office	**il Ministero degli Interni**
Ministry of Education	**il Ministero della Pubblica Istruzione**
Ministry of Defence	**il Ministero della Difesa**
the city council	**il consiglio municipale**
town hall	**il municipio**
town / city councillor	**il consigliere municipale**
mayor	**il sindaco**
constituency (area)	**il collegio elettorale**
election	**le elezioni**
the vote	**il voto / la votazione**
to speak	**parlare**
to make a speech	**fare un discorso**
to canvass	**fare propaganda elettorale**
to debate	**dibattere / discutere**
to vote	**votare**
to pay taxes	**pagare imposte / tasse**

The armed forces **Le Forze Armate**

army	**l'Esercito**
soldier / tank/ to march	**il soldato / un carro armato / marciare**
navy	**la Marina (Militare)**
sailor / warship / to sail	**il marinaio / la nave da guerra / navigare**
airforce	**l'Aviazione Militare**
airman / pilot / jet fighter /	**l'aviatore / il pilota / il caccia**

to fly	**a reazione / volare**
police force	**la polizia**
policeman / police car / to arrest	**il poliziotto / la macchina della polizia / arrestare**
war against terrorism	**la guerra contro il terrorismo**
war against organized crime	**la guerra contro la criminalità organizzata**
terrorist attack	**l'attacco terrorista**
suicide bomber	**il terrorista suicida**
sea to air missile	**il missile mare-aria**
to defend	**difendere**
to fight	**combattere**
to guard	**fare la guardia a**
to protect	**proteggere**
to spy	**spiare**

15.2 Local government and services

Core vocabulary

police	**la polizia**
emergency services	**i servizi di pronto intervento**
ambulance	**l'ambulanza**
fire brigade	**il Corpo dei Vigili del Fuoco**
telephone	**il telefono**
electricity	**l'elettricità**
gas	**il gas**
water	**l'acqua**
mayor	**il sindaco**
town hall	**il municipio**
local council	**il consiglio comunale**
roads	**le strade**
transport	**i trasporti**
tourist office	**l'ufficio turistico**
council offices	**gli uffici municipali**

telephone	**il telefono**
taxes	**le imposte**
council tax	**l'imposta comunale**
bureaucracy	**la burocrazia**
the small print	**la parte scritta in piccolo**
red tape	**le lungaggini burocratiche**
civil servant	**il funzionario**
paperwork	**l'amministrazione**
a pass	**il lasciapassare**
a permit	**un permesso**
a certificate of residence	**un permesso di soggiorno**
a receipt	**una ricevuta**
a driving licence	**una patente di guida**
insurance	**l'assicurazione**
medical insurance	**l'assicurazione medica**
medical check	**la visita medica**
solicitor / lawyer	**l'avvocato / il notaio**
criminal offence	**il reato**
court	**il tribunale / la corte**
sentence	**la sentenza / condanna**
fine	**la multa**
imprisonment	**la reclusione**

Useful phrases

I don't understand	**Non capisco**
I didn't know	**Non lo sapevo**
I have already supplied you with this document	**Le ho già fornito questo documento**
I need help	**Ho bisogno di aiuto**
Is there anyone who can help me?	**C'è qualcuno che mi possa aiutare?**
When are the offices open?	**A che ora aprono gli uffici?**
Where do I need to go to get ...?	**Dove devo andare per avere ...?**
What do I need?	**Di che cosa ho bisogno?**
Where can I get it?	**Dove posso trovarlo/la?**
a (rubber) stamp	**il timbro**

It has/hasn't been stamped	**Non è stato timbrato**

> **Insight**
>
> Italy has a very widespread and highly developed (but fortunately not very efficient!) bureaucracy, and a bewildering number of police forces and government agencies. You will probably encounter at least some of these bodies while you are there …

15.3 Money

currency	**la moneta / valuta**
dollars	**i dollari**
sterling	**la sterlina**
euros	**gli euro**
bank	**la banca**
bank account	**il conto in banca**
current account	**il conto corrente**
deposit	**il deposito**
saving account	**il libretto di risparmio**
account number	**il numero del conto**
bank sort code	**il numero di agenzia bancaria**
cash	**contanti**
a cheque	**un assegno**
cheque book	**il libretto degli assegni**
credit card	**la carta di credito**
cheque card	**la carta assegni**
signature	**la firma**
number / code	**il numero / codice**
loan	**il prestito**
overdraft	**lo scoperto di conto**
bank transfer	**il trasferimento bancario / bonifico**
in credit	**coperto**
in the red	**scoperto / in rosso**

bankruptcy	**la bancarotta**
mortgage	**il mutuo ipotecario**
household insurance	**l'assicurazione sulla casa**
to apply	**presentare domanda**
to be accepted	**essere accettato**
to be refused	**essere rifiutato**
stocks and shares	**i valori di borsa**
stock market	**la borsa**
prices	**i prezzi**
dividend	**il dividendo**
profits	**i profitti**
loss	**la perdita**
inflation	**l'inflazione**
to win	**vincere**
to lose	**perdere**
to make a gain	**guadagnare**
to make a loss	**subire una perdita**
to buy / sell shares	**comprare / vendere azioni**
to save	**risparmiare**
accounts	**i conti**
accountant	**il ragioniere / commercialista**
annual accounts	**i conti annuali**
income tax	**l'imposta sul reddito**

Insight

Italy has been a member of the eurozone since its inception, but you will still encounter the odd person who gives you a price in **lire,** or who thinks in **lire** and has to convert prices into **lire** to understand them. You will know when this is happening because the person will be talking in implausibly large numbers!

15.4 National holidays

national holidays	**le feste nazionali**
bank holidays	**i giorni di feste civili**
annual paid holidays	**le ferie**
local holidays	**le feste locali**
Christmas Eve	**la Vigilia di Natale**
Christmas Day	**Natale**
New Year's Eve	**la Vigilia di Capodanno**
New Year	**il Capodanno**
the Epiphany (6 January)	**La Befana**
Carnival	**Carnevale**
Shrove Tuesday	**Martedì grasso**
Ash Wednesday	**Mercoledì delle Ceneri**
Easter Week / Holy Week	**(la) Settimana Santa**
Good Friday	**Venerdì Santo**
Easter Sunday	**Pasqua**
Easter Monday	**Pasquetta**
Liberation Day (25 April)	**La Liberazione**
National Holiday (August 15)	**Ferragosto**
Halloween	**la vigilia di Ognissanti**
All Saints' Day	**Ognissanti**
feast of the Virgin Mary (8 December)	**L'Immacolata**
patron saint's day	**la festa del santo patrono**
village fete	**la festa del paese**
circus	**il circo**
concert	**il concerto**
band	**la banda**
gig	**la serata musicale**
festival of (music)	**il festival (di musica)**
competition	**la gara**
championship	**il campionato**
match	**la partita**
wine festival	**la sagra del vino / della vendemmia**
regional costume	**il costume regionale**
procession	**la processione**

15.5 Environmental issues

Core vocabulary

the environment	**l'ambiente**
environmentalist	**l'ambientalista**
environmental issues	**le questioni ambientali**
ecology	**l'ecologia**
ecosystem	**l'ecosistema**
erosion	**l'erosione**

Foodstuffs **I generi alimentari**

GM (genetically modified)	**geneticamente modificato**
organic	**organico**
artificial fertilizer	**il fertilizzante artificiale**
nitrates	**i nitrati**
pesticides	**il pesticida**
poison	**il veleno**
weedkiller	**l'erbicida**

Pollution **L'inquinamento**

environmental pollution	**l'inquinamento ambientale**
acid rain	**la pioggia acida**
air pollution	**l'inquinamento atmosferico**
car exhaust	**i gas di scappamento delle macchine**
detergent	**il detergente / detersivo**

biodegradable detergent	**il detergente biodegradabile**
global warming	**il riscaldamento dell'atmosfera terrestre**
greenhouse gas	**l'effetto serra**
nuclear testing	**gli esperimenti nucleari**
ozone layer	**la fascia dell'ozono**
radiation	**la radiazione**
radioactive waste	**le scorie radioattive**
water pollution	**l'inquinamento dell'acqua**

Energy **L'energia**

power	**l'elettricità / la corrente**
nuclear power	**l'energia nucleare**
hydroelectric power	**l'energia idroelettrica**
solar power	**l'energia solare**
wind power	**l'energia eolica**
power station	**la centrale elettrica**

Recycling **Il riciclaggio**

glass	**il vetro**
cans	**le scatole**
paper	**la carta**
plastic	**la plastica**
compost	**il concime**

Resources **Le risorse**

sustainable resources	**le risorse che possono essere mantenute**
renewable	**rinnovabile**
Greenpeace	**Greenpeace**
the protection	**la protezione**
of the environment	**dell'ambiente**
of animals	**degli animali**
of plants	**delle piante**
to protect	**proteggere**
to conserve	**conservare**
to destroy	**distruggere**
to dispose of	**disfarsi di**

to throw away	**buttare via / gettare**
national park	**il parco nazionale**
region of special scientific interest	**la regione di interesse scientifico speciale**
protected / conservation area	**la zona protetta**
listed building	**l'edificio protetto**
ancient monument	**il monumento storico**
archeological site	**gli scavi archeologici**

15.6 Religion

Core vocabulary

religion	**la religione**
beliefs	**le credenze**
faith	**la fede**
Buddhism	**il buddismo**
Christianity	**il cristianesimo**
Hinduism	**l'induismo**
Islam	**l'Islam**

God	**Dio**
Buddha	**Budda**
Christ	**Cristo**
Mohammed	**Maometto**
the prophet	**il profeta**

I am a / an ...	**sono ...**
agnostic	**agnostico**
atheist	**ateo**
buddhist	**buddista**
catholic	**cattolico**
Christian	**cristiano**
Hindu	**indù**
Jew	**ebreo**
Moslem	**musulmano**
Quaker	**quacchero**

Jehovah's witness	**testimone di Geova**
cathedral	**il duomo / la cattedrale**
chapel	**la cappella**
church	**la chiesa**
mosque	**la moschea**
temple	**il tempio**
religious leader	**il capo religioso**
bishop	**il vescovo**
imam	**l'imam**
monk	**il frate / monaco**
nun	**la suora / monaca**
priest	**il prete / sacerdote**
rabbi	**il rabbino**
prayer	**la preghiera**
hymn	**l'inno**
religious service	**la funzione religiosa**
mass	**la messa**
baptism, christening	**il battesimo**
(first) communion	**la (prima) comunione**
wedding	**le nozze / il matrimonio**
funeral	**il funerale**

Insight

Italy is of course the home of the Roman Catholic Church, and is a very strongly Catholic country. A lot of Italian imprecations and swear words involve the use of the word **Dio** or **Madonna,** but be very careful how you use these, because you can cause genuine shock by their careless use!

Useful verbs

to attend church	**andare in chiesa**
to believe	**credere**
to pray	**pregare**

to preach	**predicare**
to kneel	**inginocchiarsi**
to sing	**cantare / salmodiare**
to chant	**cantare**
to worship	**adorare**

15.7 Social issues

the community	**la comunità**
charity / charitable work	**le opere di carità**
charity / charitable organization	**l'organizzazione filantropica**
social services	**i servizi sociali**
social work	**l'assistenza sociale**
the quality of life	**la qualità della vita**
fundamental problems	**problemi fondamentali**
financial problems	**problemi finanziari**
poverty	**la povertà / miseria**
debt	**i debiti**
psychological problems	**i problemi psicologici**
depression	**la depressione**
emotional deprivation	**le carenze affettive**
insecurity	**l'insicurezza**
loneliness	**la solitudine**
mental health	**la salute mentale**
neglect	**la trascuratezza**
racial tension	**la tensione razziale**
stress	**lo stress / la tensione nervosa**
unemployment	**la disoccupazione**
environmental problems	**i problemi ambientali**
bad housing	**l'alloggio di bassa qualità**
family problems	**i problemi familiari**
inner city	**zona urbana in degrado**
lack of food / clean water / sewage	**la mancanza di cibo / acqua potabile / depurazione dei liquami**

TEST YOURSELF

Decipher these number codes and write down the English for the words they represent (a = 1, b = 2, etc.).

1   21 14 1 16 1 20 5 14 20 5 4 9 7 21 9 4 1
2   7 12 9 21 6 6 9 3 9 13 21 14 9 3 9 16 1 12 9
3   12 1 2 21 18 15 3 18 1 26 9 1
4   12 ' 5 19 5 18 3 9 20 15
5   9 12 19 9 14 4 1 3 15
6   12 1 6 1 18 13 1
7   9 16 18 15 2 12 5 13 9 1 13 2 9 5 14 20 1 12 5
8   12 ' 5 14 5 18 7 9 1 9 4 18 15 5 12 5 20 20 18 9 3 1
9   14 1 20 1 12 5
10 12 1 2 1 14 3 1 18 15 20 20 1

Answers:

1   una patente di guida – a driving licence
2   gli uffici municipali – the council offices
3   la burocrazia – bureaucracy
4   l'Esercito – the Army
5   il sindaco – the mayor
6   la firma – signature
7   i problemi ambientali – environmental problems
8   l'energia idroelettrica – hydroelectric power
9   Natale – Christmas
10 la bancarotta – bankruptcy

16

The media

16.1 The press

Core vocabulary

the press	**la stampa**
newspaper	**il giornale**
magazine, review	**la rivista**
comic	**il giornalino a fumetti**
daily	**quotidiano**
weekly	**settimanale**
monthly	**mensile**
bi-monthly	**bimestrale**
quarterly	**trimestrale**
yearly	**annuale**
publisher	**la casa editrice**
editor	**il redattore**
journalist	**il giornalista**
journalism	**il giornalismo**
reporter (press)	**il reporter / cronista**
reporter (TV, radio)	**il telecronista**
correspondent	**il corrispondente**
special correspondent	**il corrispondente speciale**
war correspondent	**il corrispondente di guerra**

critic	**il critico**
press agency*	**l'agenzia stampa**
Reuters	**Reuters**

*ANSA is a well-known Italian press agency.

front page	**la prima pagina**
back page	**l'ultima pagina**
headline	**il titolo**
column	**la colonna**
article	**l'articolo**
brief report	**il reportage breve**
advertisement	**la pubblicità**
TV advertisement	**lo spot**
notices	**gli annunci**
obituaries	**i necrologi**
small ads	**gli annunci economici**

News items **Le notizie**

natural disaster	**il disastro naturale**
flood	**l'inondazione**
earthquake	**il terremoto**
eruption of a volcano	**l'eruzione di un vulcano**
storm	**la tempesta**
hurricane	**l'uragano**
tornado	**il tornado**
torrential rain	**la pioggia torrenziale**
road accidents	**gli incidenti stradali**
car crash	**l'incidente d'auto**
collision	**la collisione / lo scontro**
plane crash	**incidente aereo**
a plane crashed over the Atlantic	**un aereo è precipitato sopra l'Atlantico**
boat involved in collision	**nave coinvolta in una collisione**
terrorist attack	**l'attacco terrorista**
demonstration	**la manifestazione**
strike	**lo sciopero**

a call to go on strike	**la proclamazione di sciopero**
fire	**l'incendio**
a fire started on the fourth level at 3 pm	**un incendio è scoppiato al quarto piano alle ore 15**

- Italian newspaper reports of incidents and accidents often use unexpected tenses; the present tense gives vividness to narration of incidents, and the imperfect is sometimes used with similar effect.
- The distinction in the British press between the tabloid press and the broadsheet newspapers does not exist in Italy, where most papers are of the same size – smaller than a broadsheet, but a bit larger than a tabloid paper. Of course, there are various sizes, but there is no division of style and tone as in the UK press.
- Newspapers in Italy tend to be focused on news rather than on gossip about stars and so on, which is left to magazines like *Oggi, Grazie, Ecco!* etc. As a rule, even regional papers contain lots of national and international news, as well as local news and information; as a result, many Italian people buy local rather than national papers.

16.2 Books

Core vocabulary

title	**il titolo**
author	**l'autore / l'autrice**
writer	**lo scrittore / la scrittrice**
illustrator	**l'illustratore**
cartoonist	**il cartonista (di cartoni animati)**
paperback	**il tascabile / paperback**
biography	**la biografia**
autobiography	**l'autobiografia**
novel	**il romanzo**
short story	**il racconto / la novella**
dictionary	**il dizionario / vocabolario**

encyclopaedia	**l'enciclopedia**
atlas	**l'atlante**
guide book	**la guida turistica**
(road) map book	**l'atlante stradale**
fiction	**la narrativa**
non-fiction	**tutta la prosa che non è narrativa**

The text **Il testo**

to write	**scrivere**
to edit	**curare / editare**
to print	**stampare**
to publish	**pubblicare**
to sign	**firmare**
punctuation	**la punteggiatura**
paragraph	**il paragrafo**
sentence	**la frase**
line	**la linea**
capital / upper case letter	**la maiuscola**
lower case letter	**la minuscola**
full stop	**il punto**
comma	**la virgola**
semi-colon	**il punto e virgola**
colon	**i due punti**
exclamation mark	**il punto esclamativo**
question mark	**il punto interrogativo**
hyphen	**il trattino**
dash	**la lineetta**
dot-dot-dot	**i puntini di sospensione**

Literary genres **I generi letterari**

novels	**i romanzi**
mystery novels	**i romanzi del mistero**
detective novels	**i romanzi polizieschi / gialli**
short stories	**le novelle / i racconti**
foreign literature	**la letteratura straniera**
literary review	**la critica / recensione letteraria**
poetry	**la poesia**

| epic (poetry) | il poema epico |
| epic (film) | l'epopea |

| essays | i saggi* |

*This Italian word for a literary essay cannot be used in the school/
student sense, when 'tema' or 'composizione' is used instead.

Useful phrases

What sort of books do you like to read?	Che genere di libro ti piace leggere?
Who is your favourite author?	Chi è il tuo autore preferito?
I like reading books about ...	Mi piace leggere dei libri su ...
I like reading books where ...	Mi piace leggere dei libri in cui ...
I like reading books that ...	Mi piace leggere dei libri che ...

16.3 Cinema and television

The cinema **Il cinema**

auditorium	l'auditorio / la sala
(big) screen	lo schermo (grande)
seat	il posto
foyer	il ridotto / foyer
ticket	il biglietto
booking office	la biglietteria

Types of films **Generi di film**

thriller	il thriller
love story / romance	il film d'amore
historical film	il film di storia
science fiction	il film di fantascienza
horror film	il film dell'orrore
war film	il film di guerra
comedy	la commedia
detective	il film poliziesco
drama	il film drammatico
adverts	la pubblicità

The cast and the crew **Il cast e la troupe**

a film star	**un divo del cinema**
an actor / actress	**un attore / un'attrice**
a leading role	**un ruolo di primo piano**
a supporting role	**un ruolo non di protagonista**
a singer	**un/una cantante**
a dancer	**un ballerino / una ballerina**
director	**il regista**
producer	**il produttore / la produttrice**
cameraman	**il cameraman**
sound recordist	**il tecnico del suono**

Television **La televisione**

television set	**il televisore**
small screen	**lo schermo piccolo**
cable	**televisione via cavo**
satellite	**televisione via satellite**
dish	**l'antenna parabolica**
video recorder	**il videoregistratore**
DVD recorder	**il lettore-registratore DVD**
video rental / shop	**la videoteca**
the video	**il video**
the DVD	**il DVD**
the film is dubbed / subtitled	**questo film è doppiato / ha i sottotitoli**
remote control	**il telecomando**
channel	**il canale**

The programmes **I programmi**

credits (opening / closing)	**i titoli di testa /coda**
commercials (adverts)	**gli spot**
cartoons	**i cartoni animati**
children's programmes	**i programmi per bambini**
chat show	**il talk show**
documentary	**il documentario**
feature film	**il lungometraggio**
game show	**il gioco a premi**
quiz programme	**il programma di quiz**

news programme	**il programma di notizie**
opinion programme	**un dibattito televisivo**
soap	**la telenovela / soap opera**
weather forecast	**le previsioni del tempo / il meteo**

The people **Le persone**

news reporter	**il reporter**
news reader	**l'annunciatore / l'annunciatrice**
presenter	**il presentatore / la presentatrice**
interviewer	**l'intervistatore / l'intervistatrice**
commentator	**il radiocronista / telecronista**
disc jockey	**il DJ / disc jockey**
game show host	**il presentatore di un gioco a premi**
the viewer	**il telespettatore / la telespettatrice**

Radio **La radio**

station	**la stazione**
programme	**il programma**
frequency	**la frequenza**
on FM	**FM / a modulazione di frequenza**
on LW	**in onde lunghe**
on MW	**in onde medie**

Useful verbs

to change channels	**cambiare di canale**
to turn on / off the telly	**accendere / spegnere la tivù**
to turn the sound up	**alzare il volume**
to turn the sound down	**abbassare il volume**
to broadcast	**trasmettere**
to record	**registrare**

Useful phrases

What is your favourite programme?	**Qual è il tuo programma preferito?**

Do you like documentaries?	**Ti piacciono i documentari?**
Who is your favourite presenter?	**Chi è il tuo presentatore preferito?**
He/she is partial / impartial	**(Lei/lui) è parziale / imparziale**

> ## Insight
> The Italian media are remarkably diverse, and range from a largely unregulated television network which is largely owned by one combine (at the time of writing the Mediaset empire owned by the Prime Minister, Silvio Berlusconi) to a printed press, a large proportion of which is also controlled by Mediaset, but which tends to be more conservative in its writings.

TEST YOURSELF

Work out which Italian word goes with which English word.

1	il giornale	**a**	TV ad
2	la rivista	**b**	the obituaries
3	il titolo	**c**	journalist
4	il canale	**d**	weekly
5	lo spot	**e**	the press
6	mensile	**f**	title
7	settimanale	**g**	newspaper
8	i necrologi	**h**	magazine
9	il cronista	**i**	monthly
10	la stampa	**j**	channel

Answers: 1g, 2h, 3f, 4j, 5a, 6i, 7d, 8b, 9c, 10e.

Taking it further

Books

For an introduction to Italian history, geography, language and culture, and modern-day society, try:

Teach Yourself Italian Language, Life & Culture, Derek Aust with Mike Zollo (Hodder and Stoughton, 2003).

Modern Italy 1871–1995, Martin Clark (Longman, 1996).

For those wanting more in-depth knowledge of the language:

The Italian Language Today, Anna and Giulio Lepschy (Routledge, 1988).

A Linguistic History of Italian, Martin Maiden (Longman, 1995).

Watching and listening

Satellite television is a good investment – in the UK, many Italian television stations are available on Eutelsat FII / Hotbird. In some areas, Italian channels are available on Cable TV.

Radio reception on a normal set is variable, though in some areas Italian stations can be received clearly, depending on atmospheric conditions. Many good Italian radio stations are available on Satellite TV. For Italian music, try **Radio Italia S (solo musica italiana)** on the Hotbird satellite, which only broadcasts Italian music.

If you can access Italian television or radio, listen to a variety of different types of material or programmes. Try watching or listening to the news having already seen or heard it in the English-speaking media, as many international news items will be shown on both. This will help your understanding and give you confidence.

If you are interested in opera or popular music, choose recordings with clear lyrics; in the case of opera, the names of Luciano Pavarotti and Andrea Bocelli are well known. Italian popular music features many **cantautori** – singer-song-writers – and their ballad-style songs can offer good listening practice. CDs are easily available in Italy, but a specialist music shop may also be able to help. Try some of the following: **Luigi Tenco, Gino Paoli, Fabrizio de André, Lucio Battisti, Lucio Dalla, Paolo Conte**. If you prefer more of a 'rock' style, try **Luciano Ligabue, Litfiba** and **Edoardo Bennato**. Finally, the internationally known **Zucchero (Sugar) Fornaciari** has many slowish ballads in his repertoire in which the diction is clear enough to make for pleasurable and instructive listening.

Many Italian films are available on video and DVD, most with English sub titles if you really need them!

Places to go

Look out for performances of Italian culture in local venues, for example, opera, films, art exhibitions, etc. Also watch out for Italian (speaking) films at local film clubs and on television.

Italian paintings are sometimes displayed in galleries outside Italy, including the USA and UK. Often, there are special seasons, when Italian works of art are brought for short-term exhibitions.

Reading

Obviously, this will depend on whether or not you can read Italian well enough to keep your interest going! Try short, simple items in the press, such as advertisements, small ads and short articles on well-known subjects. Another very useful source of reading material is the Internet, where there is plenty of visual material to support your understanding. Try tourist and hotel websites, or go to one which deals with your hobby or your work specialization: you will already know a lot about the topic, so even understanding new words will be easier as you are familiar with the context.

If you wish to read literature in Italian, the best approach is to go for a 'school text' if one is available, that is one which has been set for Italian literature examinations: such editions have a useful introduction, explanatory notes and glossaries.

Websites

The web is very popular in Italy and is very widely used, so there is plenty of good material available in Italian – all good practice. Choose your subject and do the necessary search, but be prepared to be bombarded with Italian. There are Italian websites available related to many of the subjects covered in this book. You can either do a search using your favourite English-language search engine, preferably one with Italian links, or if you can cope with the language enough to use an Italian search engine, go direct to one of those listed below.

Be warned: websites come and go, and their addresses often change. These were all fine at the time of going to press!

Search engines

http://www.virgilio.it
http://arianna.libero.it/

Using an Italian search engine may speed up your search for a specific Italian site.

Tourism, culture and current affairs

http://www.italyguide.com
http://www.lonelyplanet.com/destinations/europe/italy/
http://www.initaly.com
http://www.italcultur.org.uk

The press

Corriere della Sera   http://corriere.virgilio.it
Il Mattino   http://www.ilmattino.it

Language learning on the web

For basic language practice, go to:

http://www.languagesonline.org.uk
http://www.bbc.co.uk/education/languages
http://polyglot.lss.wisc.edu/lss/lang/teach.html

Italian Embassies

The Italian Embassies in London and Washington provide many services online and links to other useful Internet sites:

http://www.embitaly.org.uk
http://www.italyemb.org